MONSTERS

CRITICAL READING SERIES

MONSTERS

21 Stories of the Most Fantastic and Gruesome Creatures of All Time—with Exercises for Developing Reading Comprehension and Critical Thinking Skills

Henry Billings

Melissa Billings

Dan Dramer

JAMESTOWN PUBLISHERS

a division of NTC/CONTEMPORARY PUBLISHING GROUP
Lincolnwood, Illinois USA

ISBN 0-89061-107-6

Published by Jamestown Publishers,
a division of NTC/Contemporary Publishing Group, Inc.
4255 West Touhy Avenue,
Lincolnwood (Chicago), Illinois 60712-1975, U.S.A.
© 1999 NTC/Contemporary Publishing Group, Inc.

6 7 8 9 10 11 12 13 14 113 / 055 09 08 07 06 05 04 03

CONTENTS

UNIT THREE

To the Student

We are all fascinated by monsters. We shiver when we read about them in ancient myths and in favorite fairy tales. We cringe when we see them on the big screen in fantasy and science fiction movies. We whisper when we imagine them as we sit around a campfire in the middle of a dark forest. Monsters—creatures of extraordinary size or incredible cruelty or terrible violence—both intrigue and disgust us. Every time we think about monsters, we combine our deepest fears into one imaginative and terrifying package.

Each lesson in this book will introduce you to a different monster. Some of these monsters come down to us from ancient times, and others are hot topics in today's newspapers. Some of them are the inventions of a single writer, while others have been created and refined by groups of people over many years. You will recognize some of the monsters from books and movies, and others will be new to you.

All the articles tell about famous monsters familiar to many people. As you read and enjoy them, you will also be developing your reading skills. *Monsters* is for students who already read fairly well but who want to read faster and to increase their understanding of what they read. If you complete the 21 lessons—reading the articles and completing the exercises—you will surely increase your reading speed and improve your reading comprehension and critical thinking skills. Also, because these exercises include items of the types often found on state and national tests, learning how to complete them will prepare you for tests you may have to take in the future.

How to Use This Book

About the Book.   *Monsters* contains three units, each of which includes seven lessons. Each lesson begins with an article about an unusual event, person, or group. The article is followed by a group of four reading comprehension exercises and a set of three critical thinking exercises. The reading comprehension exercises will help you understand the article. The critical thinking exercises will help you think about what you have read and how it relates to your own experience.

At the end of each lesson, you will also have the opportunity to give your personal response to some aspect of the article and then to assess how well you understood what you read.

The Sample Lesson. Working through the sample lesson, the first lesson in the book, with your class or group will demonstrate how a lesson is organized. The sample lesson explains how to complete the exercises and score your answers. The correct answers for the sample exercises and sample scores are printed in lighter type. In some cases, explanations of the correct answers are given. The explanations will help you understand how to think through these question types.

If you have any questions about how to complete the exercises or score them, this is the time to get the answers.

Working Through Each Lesson. Begin each lesson by looking at the photographs and reading the captions. Before you read, predict what you think the article will be about. Then read the article.

Sometimes your teacher may decide to time your reading. Timing helps you keep track of and increase your reading speed. If you have been timed, enter your reading time in the box at the end of the lesson. Then use the Words-per-Minute Table to find your reading speed, and record your speed on the Reading Speed graph at the end of the unit.

Next complete the Reading Comprehension and Critical Thinking exercises. The directions for each exercise will tell you how to mark your answers. When you have finished all four Reading Comprehension exercises, use the answer key provided by your teacher to check your work. Follow the directions after each exercise to find your score. Record your Reading Comprehension scores on the graph at the end of each unit. Then check your answers to the Author's Approach, Summarizing and Paraphrasing, and Critical Thinking exercises. Fill in the Critical Thinking chart at the end of each unit with your evaluation of your work and comments about your progress.

At the end of each unit you will also complete a Compare/Contrast chart. The completed chart will help you see what the articles have in common, and it will give you an opportunity to explore your own feelings, thoughts, and attitudes about monsters.

SAMPLE LESSON

THE EVIL MR. HYDE

It was three o'clock in the morning in the heart of London. There were still many people up and about, for large cities never sleep. A dark, burly man walked quickly down a side street, paying no attention to anyone else. Coming toward him at a run was a little girl between eight and 10 years old. The two collided at the corner, and the girl fell to the ground. Then, as passersby watched in horror, the man trampled the child and left her on the ground, screaming in pain.

2   What sort of creature was this? Who would do such a despicable thing? It was the hideous and evil Mr. Hyde. The very sight of him caused disgust and fear in those who looked upon him.

3   Edward Hyde is the evil side of the good Doctor Henry Jekyll in the Robert Louis Stevenson story *The Strange Case of Dr. Jekyll and Mr. Hyde.* Written in 1886, the novel is both a thriller and a moral tale about the good and evil sides of human nature. The basis of the story is that there are two sides to every human being. One part wants to do good and help other people. The other part delights

In the years since its original publication, the story of Dr. Jekyll and Mr. Hyde has been the subject of several films and plays.

in doing evil. Stevenson, like many others of his time, believed that the two natures are constantly at war within us. The idea is that most people succeed in hiding their bad side. But in criminals, the evil side has won out.

4   In *The Strange Case of Dr. Jekyll and Mr. Hyde*, Dr. Jekyll is a good and well-respected physician. He wonders what it would be like if the two sides of human beings could be separated. Wouldn't it be wonderful to have people who were totally good? Evil could then be wiped from the face of the earth!

5   One day, while working in his laboratory, Dr. Jekyll accidentally mixes a strange drug that has the power to separate the two personalities. He drinks the drug and instantly undergoes a strange transformation. Dreadful pains rack his body. He feels that he is being twisted inside, as though his bones are grinding. A tremendous feeling of horror comes over him. But as that feeling passes, he begins to feel lighter and younger, and also reckless and wicked! Then, upon looking into a mirror, he meets Mr. Hyde for the first time. The good and handsome doctor has been transformed into a dark, hairy, twisted, disgusting creature. He has become pure evil. Frightened, he quickly swallows another dose of the drug and is relieved to find himself restored to the personality of Dr. Jekyll.

6   The good doctor soon finds that he cannot control his impulse to drink the drug and transform himself. In the guise of Mr. Hyde, he goes out again and again into the city to commit horrible acts. The evil creature cares for nothing and no one. Dr. Jekyll's friends notice that Jekyll has become cold and distant. He seems to have no time for them. Meanwhile, Mr. Hyde is enjoying his freedom. He feels no guilt. Whenever he gets into some kind of trouble, he has only to run back to the laboratory and drink some of the drug. Behold! He is once again Henry Jekyll.

7   All this goes on for several months, until Jekyll wakes up one morning to find that during the night he has turned back into Mr. Hyde! The evil side is becoming stronger. It is becoming harder and harder to regain the body of the good doctor. Jekyll is losing hold of his better half!

8   Jekyll is so frightened that for a while he stops taking the drug. He does good deeds to make up for Hyde's evil acts. He spends time with his friends. But he misses Mr. Hyde. So one night he again uses the drug. The devil that has been caged for so long is stronger than ever. That night on the streets, an elderly man happens to bump into Mr. Hyde. With a gleam in his eye and delight running through his terrible being, the beast clubs the defenseless man to death with his cane. While hanging

Julia Roberts and John Malkovich star in Mary Reilly, *a 1996 film version of the Jekyll and Hyde story.*

breathlessly over the dead man at his feet, Hyde suddenly becomes filled with terror. He flees from the scene and runs to the lab. A quick gulp of the drug, and he is once again Henry Jekyll. Never again, promises Jekyll. Never again.

9   Dr. Jekyll no longer feels the desire to become Mr. Hyde. But it is too late! Once again he begins slipping without warning into his evil side, even though he doesn't drink the drug. While sitting on a park bench, while dozing in a chair or sitting at his desk, he feels the terrible change coming over him. Looking down at his hands, he finds that they have become dark and hairy. His evil side is winning out. Finally, he is almost out of the powder with which to make the drug that enables him to return to being Dr. Jekyll. He buys more, but finds to his horror that it does not have the same effect. There was some unknown ingredient, some impurity, in the first powder that brought about the change. In disgust at the loathsome thing he is becoming, and in fear that Mr. Hyde will soon take over completely, Dr. Jekyll kills himself. In doing so, he also kills Mr. Hyde.

10   This story has fascinated people for more than a hundred years. More movie versions have been made of Dr. Jekyll and Mr. Hyde than of almost any other monster tale. Why are people so intrigued by this particular horror story? Perhaps it is because we can all see ourselves in it. Everyone struggles with decisions about right and wrong. Each of us sometimes chooses the attraction of what we know to be wrong or bad for us. Does evil begin to win out if you choose it too often? Is the evil within us truly as ugly and frightening as Mr. Hyde? Can we keep the monster inside us under control, or might it come to control us? 🍃

If you have been timed while reading this article, enter your reading time below. Then turn to the Words-per-Minute Table on page 71 and look up your reading speed (words per minute). Enter your reading speed on the graph on page 72.

Reading Time: Sample Lesson

_____ : _____
Minutes   Seconds

A | Finding the Main Idea

One statement below expresses the main idea of the article. One statement is too general, or too broad. The other statement explains only part of the article; it is too narrow. Label the statements using the following key:

M—Main Idea   **B—Too Broad**   **N—Too Narrow**

_B_   1. The idea that good and evil lived side by side in human beings was a popular notion in the 1800s, and was reflected in the writings of the time. [This statement is true, but it is *too broad*. The story is specifically about Dr. Jekyll and Mr. Hyde.]

_N_   2. Mr. Hyde was a disgusting, evil character in the popular Robert Louis Stevenson novel *The Strange Case of Dr. Jekyll and Mr. Hyde*. [This statement is *too narrow*. It tells nothing about the evil side of human nature that Mr. Hyde stood for.]

_M_   3. Mr. Hyde, a hideous and evil character in the novel *The Strange Case of Dr. Jekyll and Mr. Hyde*, was a symbol of the evil side of human nature. [This statement is the *main idea*. It tells you that the reading selection is about Mr. Hyde, and it tells you the most important fact about Mr. Hyde.]

_15_   Score 15 points for a correct M answer.

_10_   Score 5 points for each correct B or N answer.

_25_   **Total Score:** Finding the Main Idea

B | Recalling Facts

How well do you remember the facts in the article? Put an X in the box next to the answer that correctly completes each statement about the article.

1. The story of Dr. Jekyll and Mr. Hyde takes place in
   - ☐ a. Paris.
   - ☒ b. London.
   - ☐ c. New York.

2. Dr. Jekyll first tried to stop taking the drug when he
   - ☐ a. killed someone.
   - ☒ b. found himself turning into Mr. Hyde without taking the drug.
   - ☐ c. trampled a little girl in the streets.

3. Dr. Jekyll could no longer make the drug because he
   - ☐ a. could not buy the powder he needed.
   - ☐ b. could no longer return to the personality of Dr. Jekyll for long enough.
   - ☒ c. was not able to identify or duplicate the ingredient that had made the powder work in the first place.

4. Dr. Jekyll killed himself because he
   - ☒ a. had lost the ability to control Mr. Hyde.
   - ☐ b. was afraid he would no longer be able to escape into the personality of Mr. Hyde.
   - ☐ c. decided that people were basically evil.

5. The story of Jekyll and Hyde was written in the
   - ☐ a. 1700s.
   - ☒ b. 1800s.
   - ☐ c. 1920s.

Score 5 points for each correct answer.

_25_   **Total Score:** Recalling Facts

C | Making Inferences

When you combine your own experience and information from a text to draw a conclusion that is not directly stated in that text, you are making an inference. Below are five statements that may or may not be inferences based on information in the article. Label the statements using the following key:

C—Correct Inference   F—Faulty Inference

___C___ 1. Dr. Jekyll's friends did not know that he could transform himself into an evil creature. [This is a *correct* inference. You are told that his friends noticed only that Jekyll had become distant and no longer had time for them.]

___F___ 2. Dr. Jekyll had always wanted to live an evil life. [This is a *faulty* inference. Your are told at the beginning that he thought it would be wonderful to be able to separate the good from the evil, and to destroy the evil.]

___C___ 3. At first, Dr. Jekyll found his evil side attractive and enjoyable. [This is a *correct* inference. You are told that when Dr. Jekyll stopped taking the drug for a while he missed Hyde. He enjoyed the reckless feeling of evil.]

___F___ 4. Mr. Hyde had superhuman strength. [This is a *faulty* inference. Mr. Hyde's strength is never discussed.]

___F___ 5. If Dr. Jekyll had been able to make more of the drug, his good side would eventually have taken over. [This is a *faulty* inference. In the end, Mr. Hyde was taking over more and more, even though Dr. Jekyll kept taking the drug to win back his good side. Nothing indicates that that would have changed.]

Score 5 points for each correct answer.

___25___ **Total Score:** Making Inferences

D | Using Words Precisely

Each numbered sentence below contains an underlined word or phrase from the article. Following the sentence are three definitions. One definition is closest to the meaning of the underlined word. One definition is opposite or nearly opposite. Label those two definitions using the following key. Do not label the remaining definition.

C—Closest   O—Opposite or Nearly Opposite

1. Who would do such a <u>despicable</u> thing?

   ___C___ a. low and mean

   _____ b. unpredictable

   ___O___ c. honorable

2. He quickly swallowed another dose of the drug and was relieved to find himself <u>restored</u> to the personality of Dr. Jekyll.

   _____ a. compared

   ___O___ b. taken away

   ___C___ c. returned

3. The good doctor soon found that he could not control his <u>impulse</u> to drink the drug and transform himself.

   ___O___ a. unwillingness

   ___C___ b. sudden desire

   _____ c. generosity

4. Finally, he was almost out of the powder with which to make the drug that <u>enabled</u> him to return to being Dr. Jekyll.

   _____ a. questioned

   ___C___ b. allowed

   ___O___ c. prevented

5. In disgust at the <u>loathsome</u> thing he was becoming, Dr. Jekyll killed himself.

__C__   a. disgusting

__O__   b. admirable

_____   c. tall

__15__	Score 3 points for each correct C answer.
__10__	Score 2 points for each correct O answer.
__25__	**Total Score:** Using Words Precisely

Enter the four total scores in the spaces below, and add them together to find your Reading Comprehension Score. Then record your score on the graph on page 73.

Score	Question Type	Sample Lesson
__25__	Finding the Main Idea	
__25__	Recalling Facts	
__25__	Making Inferences	
__25__	Using Words Precisely	
__100__	**Reading Comprehension Score**	

Author's Approach

Put an X in the box next to the correct answer.

1. The main purpose of the first paragraph is to

☐ a. describe London in the early morning.

☒ b. show how evil Mr. Hyde was.

☐ c. compare Dr. Jekyll to Mr. Hyde.

2. What is the author's purpose in writing "The Evil Mr. Hyde"?

☒ a. To retell the reader the story and explain the theme of Robert Louis Stevenson's novel

☐ b. To convey a mood of anger

☐ c. To compare Dr. Jekyll to Mr. Hyde

3. Which of the following statements from the article best describes the appearance of Mr. Hyde?

☒ a. "The very sight of him caused disgust and fear in those who looked upon him."

☐ b. "In private, he thinks a great deal about the two sides of human nature."

☐ c. "While hanging breathlessly over the dead man at his feet, Hyde suddenly becomes filled with terror."

4. In this article, "Stevenson, like many others of his time, believed that the two natures are constantly at war within us" means

☐ a. Stevenson and others of his time enjoyed telling stories about crime.

☒ b. Stevenson and others of his time were fascinated by the good and bad parts of human nature.

☐ c. Stevenson and others of his time were against war and injustice.

__4__	Number of correct answers

Record your personal assessment of your work on the Critical Thinking Chart on page 74.

Summarizing and Paraphrasing

Follow the directions provided for question 1. Put an X in the box next to the correct answer for question 2.

1. Complete the following one-sentence summary of the article using the lettered phrases from the phrase bank below. Write the letters on the lines.

> **Phrase Bank:**
> a. Dr. Jekyll's decision to kill himself and Mr. Hyde
> b. Dr. Jekyll's experimentation with a drug that separates good from evil
> c. Mr. Hyde's increasing power over Dr. Jekyll

The article about Mr. Hyde begins with ____b____, goes on to explain ____c____, and ends with ____a____.

2. Read the statement about the article below. Then read the paraphrase of that statement. Choose the reason that best tells why the paraphrase does not say the same thing as the statement.

Statement: By repeatedly choosing something we know is wrong, we help the evil side in our nature win out over the good.

Paraphrase: People who choose evil don't know the difference between right and wrong.

☐ a. Paraphrase says too much.

☐ b. Paraphrase doesn't say enough.

☒ c. Paraphrase doesn't agree with the statement about the article.

> ____2____ Number of correct answers
>
> Record your personal assessment of your work on the Critical Thinking Chart on page 74.

Critical Thinking

Put an X in the box next to the correct answer for questions 1, 3, 4, and 5. Follow the directions provided for question 2.

1. From the article, you can predict that if Dr. Jekyll had turned into Mr. Hyde for good,

☒ a. Mr. Hyde would have hurt and killed people until someone killed him.

☐ b. Mr. Hyde would have tried to find a drug to turn him back into Dr. Jekyll.

☐ c. Dr. Jekyll's friends would have learned to like Mr. Hyde.

2. Choose from the letters below to correctly complete the following statement. Write the letters on the lines.

On the positive side, ____c____, but on the negative side ____a____.

a. Dr. Jekyll also killed himself

b. Mr. Hyde is also hairy and ugly

c. Dr. Jekyll killed Mr. Hyde

3. What was the cause of Dr. Jekyll's decision to take the drug again after stopping for a while?

☒ a. Dr. Jekyll missed Mr. Hyde.

☐ b. Mr. Hyde beat a man to death.

☐ c. Dr. Jekyll was afraid that he was losing hold of his better half.

4. Of the following theme categories, which would this story fit into?

☐ a. Some people are born evil.

☒ b. People constantly struggle with the good and bad sides of their natures.

☐ c. Good always triumphs over evil.

5. What did you have to do to answer question 3?

☐ a. find a list (a number of things)

☐ b. find a definition (what something means)

☒ c. find a cause (why something happened)

_____5_____ Number of correct answers

Record your personal assessment of your work on the Critical Thinking Chart on page 74.

Before reading this article, I already knew

[You might tell what you already knew about the story of Dr.

Jekyll and Mr. Hyde.]

_____

_____

Personal Response

Describe a time when you were tempted to do something that you knew was wrong.

[You might explain your decision and its consequences.]

_____

_____

_____

Self-Assessment

To get the most out of the Critical Reading series program, you need to take charge of your own progress in improving your reading comprehension and critical thinking skills. Here are some of the features that help you work on those essential skills.

Reading Comprehension Exercises.   Complete these exercises immediately after reading the article. They help you recall what you have read, understand the stated and implied main ideas, and add words to your working vocabulary.

Critical Thinking Skills Exercises.   These exercises help you focus on the author's approach and purpose, recognize and generate summaries and paraphrases, and identify relationships between ideas.

Personal Response and Self-assessment.   Questions in this category help you relate the articles to your personal experience and give you the opportunity to evaluate your understanding of the information in that lesson.

Compare and Contrast Charts.   At the end of each unit you will complete a Compare and Contrast chart. The completed chart helps you see what the articles have in common and gives you an opportunity to explore your own ideas about the topics discussed in the articles.

The Graphs.   The graphs and charts at the end of each unit enable you to keep track of your progress. Check your graphs regularly with your teacher. Decide whether your progress is satisfactory or whether you need additional work on some skills. What types of exercises are you having difficulty with? Talk with your teacher about ways to work on the skills in which you need the most practice.

UNIT ONE

THE CYCLOPS

In this illustration, Ulysses hides himself beneath a ram to escape from the cave of Polyphemus the Cyclops.

It was almost 3,000 years ago that the Greek epic poet Homer wrote his great tale of adventure, *The Odyssey*. His hero is Ulysses, king of Ithaca. After fighting for Greece in the Trojan War, Ulysses and his men try to return home. They meet many obstacles along the way.

2   At one point in their journey, the Greek warriors came upon an unknown island in the Aegean Sea. When he saw the island, Ulysses decided to stop and explore. His ships were running low on supplies, and Ulysses hoped he could stock up with provisions from the island. Besides, his men were tired. They had just finished fighting a war against the Trojans and were in need of a rest. Also, being a great adventurer, Ulysses wanted to see what kind of people lived on the island.

3   The ships anchored in the harbor of the island, and most of the men stayed on board to relax. Ulysses took 12 crew members and went ashore. They carried jugs of a very special wine as gifts for the natives.

4   In those days, it was the custom for people to show hospitality to travelers. Ulysses, therefore, expected a warm welcome from the inhabitants of the

island. What he did not know, however, was that this land was the home of the Cyclopes (seye-CLO-peez). The Cyclopes were a race of giants who were primitive and cruel. In the ancient Greek language, *cyclops* meant "round eye." And indeed, each giant on the island had just one round eye, right in the middle of his forehead. The Cyclopes lived on plants that grew wild on their island. They raised giant goats and sheep that provided them with milk and cheese. And contrary to what Ulysses expected, the Cyclopes did not welcome visitors. In fact, they thought nothing of killing any strangers who ventured onto their island.

5   Because Ulysses did not know the manner of people he was about to encounter, he and his 12 companions roamed the island freely. They did not run into any Cyclopes, but they did stumble upon one of the giants' homes. It was a huge cave dug in the side of a hill. When Ulysses and his men entered it, they found gigantic pails, bowls of milk, and plates of cheese. The men were still marveling at the size of these things when they heard a noise at the mouth of the cave.

6   Turning quickly, they saw a dirty, shaggy mountain of a man standing in the entrance. It was the Cyclops Polyphemus (PAHL-uh-FEE-mus), the giant who lived there. The brute was clothed in the greasy skins of sheep, and the eye in the center of his forehead was bulging. He was holding an immense bundle of firewood, which he dropped near the mouth of the cave. Then he began to drive his giant sheep into the cave. He was so busy with his work that he didn't notice the Greeks who huddled in silence near the back of the cave. When Polyphemus had herded all his animals into the cave, he too stepped inside. Then he rolled an enormous stone across the entrance, trapping the sheep in the cave for the night. Although he did not realize it, his barricade trapped Ulysses and his 12 companions, as well.

7   The Greeks hiding in the shadows could only hope that the Cyclops would not spot them. After the giant had milked his ewes, however, he lit a fire, and in the light he immediately caught sight of the Greeks. In a great growling voice, he demanded to know the identity of these men who had dared to come, uninvited, into his home. Ulysses answered the Cyclops most politely. He explained that he and his men were Greeks on their way home from battle. In the name of the gods, he asked for the hospitality granted every traveler.

8   Polyphemus did not respond to Ulysses' request. Instead, he grabbed up two of the Greeks and hurled them against the floor of the cave, shattering them. As Ulysses and the 10 remaining men watched in horror, Polyphemus devoured the broken bodies of their comrades. He followed his gory meal with a long drink of milk, then stretched out on the floor and fell fast asleep.

9   Ulysses' first impulse was to run his sword through the body of the sleeping

A marble bust of the Cyclops Polyphemus from the second century B.C.

giant, but he fought back the temptation. He realized that if he killed the Cyclops now, he would never be able to get out of the cave. The rock that blocked the entrance was much too heavy for Ulysses and his men to move. For the moment, at least, there was nothing Ulysses could do.

10   The next morning, Polyphemus killed and ate two more of the Greeks. Again Ulysses and the others were helpless to stop him. After his feast of human flesh, the Cyclops moved the rock and herded his sheep out of the cave. Then, from outside, he rolled the rock back into place.

11   With the Cyclops out of the cave for the day, Ulysses and his companions went to work. Ulysses had thought of a plan for escape. On the floor of the cave was a large tree trunk. Polyphemus had brought it in to make a walking stick, but Ulysses had other ideas. The Greeks cut off a section of the trunk, and all that day they worked with their swords to sharpen one end to a point.

12   That night when Polyphemus returned to the cave with his flock, the tree trunk was out of sight. Polyphemus lit a fire, and then he saw Ulysses coming forward with a jug of wine. Ulysses offered the wine to the Cyclops, explaining that it was a gift. Polyphemus drank from the jug and was delighted with the wine.

13   "Tell me your name," said Polyphemus, "so that I may know who has given me this wonderful present." The wily Ulysses did not want to tell Polyphemus his real name, so he answered, "Nobody is my name. Nobody is what my parents named me."

14   "Well, Nobody, I have a gift for you too," Polyphemus said. "I shall save you until the end. You will be the last Greek I eat!" After saying those words, the Cyclops scooped up two more of Ulysses' crew members. The giant watched them squirm like puppies in his huge fist, then he popped them into his mouth and ate them. Next he drank down the wine that Ulysses had offered him. He soon fell sound asleep.

15   As the Cyclops lay unconscious on the stone floor, Ulysses seized the tree trunk by its dull end. With his men helping him, he plunged the sharpened end into the fire. When the point glowed red, Ulysses and his men drove the glowing point into the sleeping giant's eye. Before the startled Cyclops could pull the blazing tree trunk from his eye, the Greeks spun it around the eye socket several times. When Polyphemus finally pulled it loose, he was completely blinded. He bellowed in pain.

16   Other Cyclopes in nearby caves heard Polyphemus screaming. They called out to him, "Who is hurting you? You yell as if somebody is killing you."

17   "Nobody is hurting me. Nobody is killing me!" cried Polyphemus.

18   The other Cyclopes called back, "If nobody is hurting you and nobody is killing you, there is no way we can help." With that, the other Cyclopes went back to sleep.

19   When morning came, the giant sheep were eager to leave the cave for their pasture. Polyphemus rolled the stone from the mouth of the cave. But then he sat down in the entrance, his arms and legs spread wide. He would let out his flock,

but he was not going to let the Greeks get away.

20   Ulysses had anticipated that move. He had a plan for getting by the giant. Taking some rope, he tied the sheep together, side-by-side, in groups of three. Then he instructed his men to each cling to the belly of a sheep in the middle of a trio. Ulysses himself hung under the belly of the largest sheep, which was not attached to any others. As the groups of sheep headed out of he cave, the blinded Cyclops felt each one. When he felt nothing but their woolly backs he let them pass. He was convinced that the Greeks were still hiding in the cave.

21   As soon as Ulysses and his men were safely out of the cave, they let go of the sheep and ran for their ship. When they arrived, the crew on board was overjoyed. The men on the ships had almost given up hope of seeing their leader or their friends again. Ulysses quickly gave the command to sail, and the Greeks headed for home. 🍃

If you have been timed while reading this article, enter your reading time below. Then turn to the Words-per-Minute Table on page 71 and look up your reading speed (words per minute). Enter your reading speed on the graph on page 72.

Reading Time: Lesson 1

_____ : _____
Minutes   Seconds

A Finding the Main Idea

One statement below expresses the main idea of the article. One statement is too general, or too broad. The other statement explains only part of the article; it is too narrow. Label the statements using the following key:

M—Main Idea　　　**B—Too Broad**　　　**N—Too Narrow**

_____ 1. The Cyclops trapped Ulysses and his 12 companions and began eating them, but Ulysses finally outsmarted the giant and escaped with six of his men.

_____ 2. Ulysses and 12 of his men met with great danger on the island of the Cyclopes.

_____ 3. Ulysses and his men drove a burning spike into the eye of the Cyclops Polyphemus and blinded him.

_____ Score 15 points for a correct M answer.

_____ Score 5 points for each correct B or N answer.

_____ **Total Score:** Finding the Main Idea

B Recalling Facts

How well do you remember the facts in the article? Put an X in the box next to the answer that correctly completes each statement about the article.

1. The Cyclops herded
   □ a. cows.
   □ b. wild pigs.
   □ c. goats and sheep.

2. How many Greeks did Polyphemus eat?
   □ a. twelve
   □ b. six
   □ c. four

3. What did Ulysses give to Polyphemus?
   □ a. wine
   □ b. cheese
   □ c. milk

4. Polyphemus's gift to Ulysses was
   □ a. a promise to kill him last.
   □ b. a greasy sheepskin.
   □ c. some wine.

5. Ulysses and his men escaped by
   □ a. riding on the backs of sheep.
   □ b. covering themselves with sheepskins.
   □ c. clinging to the bellies of sheep.

Score 5 points for each correct answer.

_____ **Total Score:** Recalling Facts

C | Making Inferences

When you combine your own experience and information from a text to draw a conclusion that is not directly stated in that text, you are making an inference. Below are five statements that may or may not be inferences based on information in the article. Label the statements using the following key:

C—Correct Inference   F—Faulty Inference

_____ 1. Ulysses had no fear of the Cyclops.

_____ 2. The other Cyclopes would have helped Polyphemus when he was being attacked by the Greeks if they had understood that "Nobody" was a person.

_____ 3. Polyphemus was very smart as well as very strong.

_____ 4. Ulysses' plan would not have worked if Polyphemus had had two eyes.

_____ 5. Ulysses gave Polyphemus the wine in order to get him drunk and sleepy.

Score 5 points for each correct answer.

_____ **Total Score:** Making Inferences

D | Using Words Precisely

Each numbered sentence below contains an underlined word or phrase from the article. Following the sentence are three definitions. One definition is closest to the meaning of the underlined word. One definition is opposite or nearly opposite. Label those two definitions using the following key. Do not label the remaining definition.

C—Closest   O—Opposite or Nearly Opposite

1. Ulysses, therefore, expected a warm welcome from the <u>inhabitants</u> of the island.

_____ a. residents

_____ b. diameter

_____ c. visitors

2. And <u>contrary to</u> what Ulysses expected, the Cyclopes did not welcome visitors.

_____ a. after

_____ b. just the same as

_____ c. opposite to

3. Because Ulysses did not know the manner of people he was about to <u>encounter,</u> he and his 12 companions roamed the island freely.

_____ a. feed

_____ b. meet

_____ c. avoid

4. He followed his <u>gory</u> meal with a long drink of milk, then stretched out on the floor and fell fast asleep.

_____ a. sweet, pure

_____ b. large

_____ c. bloody and horrible

5. Ulysses had <u>anticipated</u> that move.

_____ a. expected

_____ b. made

_____ c. been unprepared for

_____ Score 3 points for each correct C answer.

_____ Score 2 points for each correct O answer.

_____ **Total Score:** Using Words Precisely

Enter the four total scores in the spaces below, and add them together to find your Reading Comprehension Score. Then record your score on the graph on page 73.

Score	Question Type	Lesson 1
_____	Finding the Main Idea	
_____	Recalling Facts	
_____	Making Inferences	
_____	Using Words Precisely	
_____	**Reading Comprehension Score**	

Author's Approach

Put an X in the box next to the correct answer.

1. The main purpose of the first paragraph is to

☐ a. introduce Ulysses to the reader.

☐ b. inform the reader about the Greek poet Homer.

☐ c. describe the Trojan War.

2. From the statements below, choose those that you believe the author would agree with.

☐ a. Ulysses let the Cyclops devour some of his men because he was afraid of the monster.

☐ b. Ulysses outsmarted Polyphemus.

☐ c. The Cyclopes did not believe in granting hospitality to travelers.

3. From the statement "The wily Ulysses did not want to tell Polyphemus his real name, so he answered, 'Nobody is my name,'" you can conclude that the author wants the reader to think that

☐ a. Ulysses' real name was Nobody.

☐ b. Ulysses didn't like to give his name to strangers.

☐ c. Ulysses intended to trick Polyphemus.

4. In this article, "Ulysses' first impulse was to run his sword through the body of the sleeping giant, but he fought back the temptation" means that Ulysses wanted to

☐ a. run away from Polyphemus, but he managed to overcome his fear.

☐ b. stab Polyphemus, but he controlled himself.

☐ c. go to sleep, but he fought the urge.

_____ Number of correct answers

Record your personal assessment of your work on the Critical Thinking Chart on page 74.

CRITICAL THINKING

Summarizing and Paraphrasing

Follow the directions provided for question 1. Put an X in the box next to the correct answer for question 2.

1. Look for the important ideas and events in paragraphs 19 and 20. Summarize those paragraphs in one or two sentences.

_____

_____

_____

2. Choose the best one-sentence paraphrase for the following sentence from the article:

   "Before the startled Cyclops could pull the blazing tree trunk from his eye, the Greeks spun it around the eye socket several times."

   ☐ a. The Greeks twisted the burning tree trunk several times before the surprised Cyclops could pull it out of his eye.

   ☐ b. The Greeks ran around the startled Cyclops several times before he could pull the burning tree trunk from his eye.

   ☐ c. The Greeks spun the startled Cyclops several times before he removed the burning tree trunk from his eye.

_____ Number of correct answers

Record your personal assessment of your work on the Critical Thinking Chart on page 74.

CRITICAL THINKING

Critical Thinking

Put an X in the box next to the correct answer for questions 1 and 4. Follow the directions provided for the other questions.

1. From the information in paragraph 19, you can conclude that

   ☐ a. Polyphemus forgot about Ulysses and his men after he let his sheep out.

   ☐ b. Ulysses and his men planned to steal the monster's sheep.

   ☐ c. Polyphemus was furious when he discovered that Ulysses and his men had escaped.

2. Choose from the letters below to correctly complete the following statement. Write the letters on the lines.

   On the positive side, _____, but on the negative side _____.

   a. the Cyclops drank Ulysses' wine

   b. Ulysses figured out a way to escape from the Cyclops

   c. the Cyclops ate six of his men

3. Choose from the letters below to correctly complete the following statement. Write the letters on the lines.

   According to the article, _____ caused Ulysses to _____, and the effect was _____.

   a. stop and explore the unknown island

   b. he and his men became trapped by Polyphemus

   c. low supplies

4. Of the following theme categories, which would this story fit into?

   ☐ a. Never travel to unknown places.

   ☐ b. Intelligence can overcome brute strength.

   ☐ c. Always treat visitors with hospitality.

5. Which paragraphs from the article provide evidence that supports your answer to question 3?

_____

_____ Number of correct answers

Record your personal assessment of your work on the Critical Thinking Chart on page 74.

I'm proud of how I answered question # _____ in section _____ because

_____

_____

_____

_____

Personal Response

If you had been one of Ulysses' men, what would you have done after Polyphemus killed and ate the first two men?

_____

_____

_____

_____

KING KONG

A movie poster from the 1933 film King Kong

The gigantic ape stands atop the Empire State Building in the middle of New York City. In his hand he holds a beautiful woman. Moving gently, he places the woman on a window ledge, the safest spot he can find. Then he turns to bravely face the approaching airplanes. He knows the pilots of the planes are out to kill him, but he will not surrender. After all, he is Kong—King Kong, the most powerful creature ever born.

2   When Kong was living on his own tropical island, he truly was a king. He ruled over every creature in the jungle. Then humans landed on the island. When they discovered the huge ape, they saw not a proud and magnificent creature, but a chance for fame and fortune. They placed Kong in chains and took him to New York, where he was put on public display. People stared at and mocked him.

3   Now Kong has broken free from his bonds. He has taken the woman he loves and has climbed to the top of the tallest building in the world, hoping to escape from the men who are trying to recapture him. But as the airplanes move in, Kong sees that there is no escape. The only thing he can do is hold his ground and fight back.

4   When the planes begin their attack, Kong raises one of his giant arms and tries

to swat them away. But they move too quickly. Their guns spray a shower of bullets at Kong and then the planes zoom out of his reach. From the sidewalk below, the people of New York watch as the bullets tear into the gorilla's enormous furry body. Again and again the planes swoop in and fire their deadly bursts. Each time, they are able to fly away before Kong can grab them. He swings his arms frantically, trying desperately to fend off his attackers. But when the movie camera zooms in for a close-up, we see that hundreds of bullets have already pierced the ape's thick hide. Blood pours from wounds all over his body. It appears that the great Kong has lost the battle.

5   But then, in one swift movement, Kong manages to reach out and grab a plane. As his giant fist closes around it, we hear the crunch of glass and metal. Although we know that there is a pilot trapped inside the airplane, we do not care. We are too caught up in Kong's struggle for survival. We find ourselves rooting for him to destroy the men who are his enemies. When he crushes the airplane and defiantly flings it away, we cheer. For a moment we feel that Kong is once again king.

6   But his triumph is all too brief. Not even the mighty Kong can withstand the power of modern weapons. As more and more bullets tear into his body, the great beast weakens and sways. His blood seeps out from the gashes in his body. Finally Kong topples to the pavement far below with a tremendous, earth-shattering thud. Kong's great heart continues to beat for just one more moment, before becoming forever still.

7   So ends the story of King Kong. The movie that portrays the story of King Kong leaves the audience mourning for the fallen ape. And that is exactly what the creator of the movie wanted. His name was Merian C. Cooper. Cooper got the idea for the King Kong movie in 1929 when he was in Africa. He was there to photograph animals for another film. During his stay, however, he became interested in gorillas. He decided to make a movie about a giant ape with superior intelligence running amok on the streets of a big city.

8   Cooper initially intended to film the movie in Africa. But a friend in the movie industry introduced him to a man named Willis O'Brien, who had built many animal models and jungle landscapes for movies. When Cooper saw O'Brien's work, he was greatly impressed. He was so impressed, in fact, that he decided to film *King Kong* in a studio, using O'Brien's models and landscapes.

9   Work on the picture began in 1932. Because it required the use of numerous special effects, it was a difficult and time-consuming movie to make. Cooper had to animate the models of Kong and the other jungle animals. He also had to find a way to animate doll-sized figures of humans that were used in place of actors in some of the scenes. The dolls were used with the Kong model, which was about the size of a person, to make the ape appear

The King Kong story had been told years earlier as the popular story Beauty and the Beast.

gigantic in comparison to humans. In some scenes, for instance, Kong grabbed the tiny "people" in what appeared to be a huge paw. The people models were 16 inches tall and made of rubber and sponge. Kong's shaggy fur was a covering of dyed lambskin. The core of each model was a jointed metal frame. The joints allowed the model to be set in different positions.

10   Action was photographed by shooting a single frame, then moving the joints slightly and taking another picture, and so on. Sometimes a model was moved as little as a quarter of an inch for each shot. It took dozens of such move-and-shoot pictures just to complete a single movement such as the swinging of an arm or the taking of a step. Although the models were finely detailed, Cooper felt they weren't quite realistic enough for close shots. So for close-ups he used a huge model of Kong's head and hand, with real actors.

11   It took one year and $650,000 to make *King Kong*. At that time, that was a tremendous amount of money to spend on a film. Most of the money went for special effects, and the investment paid off. When the move-and-shoot pictures were projected on the screen, they looked amazingly lifelike. The close-ups of Kong's head and hand looked so real they were frightening. As word of the movie spread, audiences flocked to movie theaters to see it. The film was so successful that other producers decided to cash in on the theme of sympathetic apes. Eventually

there was a whole series of films about giant apes. Among them were *Son of Kong* (1933), *Mighty Joe Young* (1949), *King Kong versus Godzilla* (1962), and *King Kong Escapes* (1967).

12   In 1976, when the original *King Kong* was 43 years old, a new version of the picture was made. The story remained essentially unchanged. The new *King Kong* simply brought the old film up to date. In 1976 the Empire State Building was no longer the tallest building in the world— the twin towers of Manhattan's World Trade Center were taller. So the new film had Kong climb one of those towers. The remake also replaced the little biplanes that buzzed around Kong with helicopter gunships. The World War I machine guns of the first film became 20-millimeter cannons whose revolving barrels spit thousands of bullets per second.

13   The modern weapons rip bigger, bloodier holes in Kong, but the effect on both ape and audience remains the same. Kong still fights heroically against the deadly weapons of humans. The audience cheers when Kong grabs and destroys a helicopter that ventures too close to his great arms. And of course, in the end, the great Kong collapses and dies.

14   A lot of people who are familiar with the original *King Kong* are disappointed that the new version does not end with the same words as the original. In the first film, as Kong lies dead on the pavement, reporters gather around his body. Carl Denham, the man who captured Kong in the jungle and brought him to New York,

also stands over the body. Denham knows that it was Kong's love for the beautiful woman that led to his capture and, ultimately, to his death. So as he gazes at Kong's pitiful remains, Denham says, "That's your story, boys. It was Beauty killed the Beast."

15   In many ways, that's what *King Kong* is—the story of Beauty and the Beast. It is the idea of the beast falling hopelessly in love with the beauty that makes our hearts go out to poor Kong. In the classic story of *Beauty and the Beast*, the hideous beast that loves the beautiful girl turns into a handsome prince in the end. The two then go off together to live happily ever after. In *King Kong*, too, the beautiful woman goes off with a handsome man to live happily ever after. But the man is someone who helped to rescue the woman from the great ape. The poor Beast lives on only in the memories of movie fans. 🍃

If you have been timed while reading this article, enter your reading time below. Then turn to the Words-per-Minute Table on page 71 and look up your reading speed (words per minute). Enter your reading speed on the graph on page 72.

Reading Time: **Lesson 2**

_____ : _____
Minutes   Seconds

A Finding the Main Idea

One statement below expresses the main idea of the article. One statement is too general, or too broad. The other statement explains only part of the article; it is too narrow. Label the statements using the following key:

M—Main Idea   **B—Too Broad**   **N—Too Narrow**

_____ 1. *King Kong*, whose story is patterned after the classic story of *Beauty and the Beast*, is one of the most successful monster movies of all time.

_____ 2. A remake of *King Kong* in 1976 stuck very close to the original version made in 1933.

_____ 3. *King Kong* has continued to capture people's hearts and imaginations for over 50 years.

_____ Score 15 points for a correct M answer.

_____ Score 5 points for each correct B or N answer.

_____ **Total Score:** Finding the Main Idea

B Recalling Facts

How well do you remember the facts in the article? Put an X in the box next to the answer that correctly completes each statement about the article.

1. In the story, King Kong is captured from his home
   - ☐ a. in Polynesia.
   - ☐ b. in Africa.
   - ☐ c. on an island.

2. Merian Cooper got the inspiration for King Kong while he was in
   - ☐ a. Willis O'Brien's studio.
   - ☐ b. Africa.
   - ☐ c. a zoo.

3. The figure of King Kong was
   - ☐ a. a trained gorilla.
   - ☐ b. an animated model of a gorilla.
   - ☐ c. a person in a gorilla costume.

4. In the remake of the movie, King Kong fights his final battle from atop the
   - ☐ a. Sears Tower.
   - ☐ b. World Trade Center.
   - ☐ c. Empire State Building.

5. The 1976 film differed from the original in
   - ☐ a. the last words that were spoken.
   - ☐ b. the way in which Kong met his death.
   - ☐ c. the audience's reaction to the movie.

Score 5 points for each correct answer.

_____ **Total Score:** Recalling Facts

C | Making Inferences

When you combine your own experience and information from a text to draw a conclusion that is not directly stated in that text, you are making an inference. Below are five statements that may or may not be inferences based on information in the article. Label the statements using the following key:

C—Correct Inference   **F—Faulty Inference**

_____ 1. People continue to like *King Kong* because the story is one that people of all times and places can relate to.

_____ 2. The ape movies that followed *King Kong* were tremendously successful.

_____ 3. *King Kong* made a lot of money for the studio that produced it.

_____ 4. The special effects used in the original *King Kong* were as convincing as any modern effects could be.

_____ 5. *King Kong* is the most successful monster movie ever made.

Score 5 points for each correct answer.

_____ **Total Score:** Making Inferences

D | Using Words Precisely

Each numbered sentence below contains an underlined word or phrase from the article. Following the sentence are three definitions. One definition is closest to the meaning of the underlined word. One definition is opposite or nearly opposite. Label those two definitions using the following key. Do not label the remaining definition.

C—Closest   **O—Opposite or Nearly Opposite**

1. But when the movie camera zooms in for a close-up, we see that hundreds of bullets have already <u>pierced</u> the ape's thick hide.

_____ a. been removed from

_____ b. revealed

_____ c. penetrated

2. Cooper <u>initially</u> intended to film the movie in Africa.

_____ a. at first

_____ b. in the end

_____ c. probably

3. The audience cheers when Kong grabs and destroys a helicopter that <u>ventures</u> too close to his great arms.

_____ a. avoids approaching

_____ b. explodes

_____ c. dares to go

4. Not even the mighty Kong can <u>withstand</u> the power of modern weapons.

_____ a. resist

_____ b. understand

_____ c. give in to

5. Denham knows that it was Kong's love for the beautiful woman that led to his capture and, <u>ultimately</u>, to his death.

_____ a. finally

_____ b. amazingly

_____ c. originally

_____ Score 3 points for each correct C answer.

_____ Score 2 points for each correct O answer.

_____ **Total Score:** Using Words Precisely

Enter the four total scores in the spaces below, and add them together to find your Reading Comprehension Score. Then record your score on the graph on page 73.

Score	Question Type	Lesson 2
_____	Finding the Main Idea	
_____	Recalling Facts	
_____	Making Inferences	
_____	Using Words Precisely	
_____	**Reading Comprehension Score**	

Author's Approach

Put an X in the box next to the correct answer.

1. The author uses the first sentence of the article to
   - ☐ a. inform the reader about the Empire State Building and New York City.
   - ☐ b. describe the setting of King Kong's final scene.
   - ☐ c. tell the reader where King Kong came from.

2. Which of the following statements from the article best describes King Kong?
   - ☐ a. "After all, he is Kong—King Kong, the most powerful creature ever born."
   - ☐ b. "The close-ups of Kong's head and hand looked so real they were frightening."
   - ☐ c. "They placed Kong in chains and took him to New York, where he was put on public display."

3. In this article, "'It was Beauty killed the Beast'" means
   - ☐ a. King Kong died because he killed a beautiful woman.
   - ☐ b. a beautiful woman shot and killed King Kong.
   - ☐ c. King Kong died because he fell in love with a beautiful woman.

4. Choose the statement below that best describes the author's position in paragraph 5.
   - ☐ a. Audiences cheer for King Kong because he is a hero.
   - ☐ b. King Kong is a monster that has to be stopped.
   - ☐ c. The airplane pilot dies a tragic death.

_____ Number of correct answers

Record your personal assessment of your work on the Critical Thinking Chart on page 74.

CRITICAL THINKING

Summarizing and Paraphrasing

Put an X in the box next to the correct answer.

1. Below are summaries of the article. Choose the summary that says all the most important things about the article.

☐ a. The 1933 movie *King Kong* inspired a whole series of films about giant apes.

☐ b. In the 1933 movie *King Kong*, the giant ape is portrayed as a hero who fights to keep the woman he loves. The audience's sympathy for the beast—and the painstaking special effects in the movie—made King Kong one of the best-loved monsters of all times.

☐ c. In both movie versions about King Kong, the giant ape is portrayed as a hero.

2. Read the statement about the article below. Then read the paraphrase of that statement. Choose the reason that best tells why the paraphrase does not say the same thing as the statement.

Statement: Many people were disappointed with the remake of *King Kong* because the newer version doesn't end with Carl Denham's comment on Kong's downfall.

Paraphrase: Many people prefer the earlier version of *King Kong* to its remake because the newer version doesn't conclude with the comment made by Carl Denham, Kong's capturer, that Beauty killed the Beast.

☐ a. Paraphrase says too much.

☐ b. Paraphrase doesn't say enough.

☐ c. Paraphrase doesn't agree with the statement about the article.

_____ Number of correct answers

Record your personal assessment of your work on the Critical Thinking Chart on page 74.

Critical Thinking

Follow the directions provided for questions 1 and 3. Put an X in the box next to the correct answer for the other questions.

1. For each statement below, write O if it expresses an opinion and write F if it expresses a fact.

_____ a. The 1976 version of *King Kong* is a better movie than the original.

_____ b. Special effects make movies more enjoyable.

_____ c. The Empire State Building is no longer the tallest building in the world.

2. From the article, you can predict that if King Kong had been portrayed as a vicious killer,

☐ a. the giant ape would have won Beauty's heart.

☐ b. everyone would still consider him a hero.

☐ c. audiences wouldn't have mourned his death.

3. Using what is told about the two film versions of *King Kong* in the article, name three ways the original film is similar to and different from the remake. Cite the paragraph number(s) where you found details in the article to support your conclusions.

Similarities

_____

_____

_____

Differences

_____

_____

_____

4. What was the effect of the film's success in 1933?

☐ a. A series of films about giant apes were made.

☐ b. People sympathized with the giant ape.

☐ c. The special effects in the film looked amazingly lifelike.

5. If you were a filmmaker, how could you use the information in the article to create a sympathetic monster?

☐ a. Show the monster destroying people.

☐ b. Have the monster fall hopelessly in love.

☐ c. Have the monster climb the tallest building in the world.

_____ Number of correct answers

Record your personal assessment of your work on the Critical Thinking Chart on page 74.

Personal Response

I know how King Kong felt when everyone started attacking him because

_____

_____

_____

_____

Self-Assessment

One good question about this article that was not asked would be

_____

_____

_____

_____

and the answer is

_____

_____

_____

_____

MEDUSA

Medusa was one of the three Gorgons from Greek mythology. The Gorgons were sisters who, when gazed upon, could turn a person to stone. Medusa was the only one of the three who was mortal. This painting by Leonardo da Vinci is titled Head of Medusa.

The king's lips curled up into a cruel smile. King Polydectes, a mythical ruler in ancient Greece, was intensely pleased with himself. For a long time he had been trying to think of a way to kill a young man named Perseus. The king wanted to marry Perseus's beautiful mother, but he was afraid Perseus would stand in his way. Now, at last, he thought he had found a way to get rid of Perseus. He was confident that he had planned the perfect crime.

2   The king's plan was to ask Perseus to go on a mission to prove his courage and manliness. The mission would be to seek out and kill a monster named Medusa (muh-DOO-suh). Many men had tried to kill Medusa, but all had been destroyed by her. The king was sure that Perseus, too, would lose his life to the monster. The plan was perfect because Perseus would die but no one would accuse the king of being a murderer. Everyone would simply think that Perseus had gotten himself killed while trying to be a hero.

3   The wicked king summoned Perseus to his castle and pretended to be friendly. He put his arm around the young man's shoulders. "Perseus," he said, "at some point, all men must find a way to prove their courage. I have a challenge for you that will allow you to do this. Your challenge is to slay Medusa and bring me her head. Her head will be proof to everyone of your bravery."

4   When Perseus heard the king's challenge, he was frightened. He knew all about Medusa. She was the fiercest of all monsters. Once she had been a beautiful maiden. But she had angered the gods. In their wrath, they had turned her into a hideous monster. Now she had long, curved claws, powerful wings, and sharp fangs. For hair, she had a mass of hissing, snarling snakes that were constantly coiling and striking. But deadliest of all was her face. It was so full of evil that anyone who looked at it was instantly turned to stone. Although Perseus was nervous as he contemplated all this, he did not want to seem like a coward. He said bravely, "I will bring you Medusa's head." The king was delighted. His plan was working.

5   As Perseus set out on his mission, there was little chance that he would succeed. Luckily, Zeus, king of the gods, was aware of the king's scheme. Zeus called on the other gods to help Perseus. Hermes, swiftest of the gods, gave Perseus a pair of wings for his feet, so that he could travel quickly. The goddess Athena gave him a shield with a mirrorlike surface. "When you reach Medusa," Athena explained, "look only at her reflection in the shield. If you gaze directly at her, you will be turned to stone."

6   Armed with the wings and the shield, Perseus quickly made his way to the land where Medusa lived. Along the last few

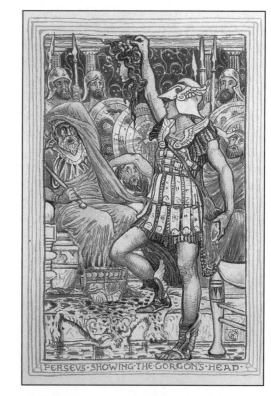

An illustration from a book of myths from 1892 depicts Perseus showing the head of Medusa to King Polydectes.

miles, he saw many men who had been turned to stone. They stood frozen in place for all time. When at last he reached the hollow where the monster lived, Perseus saw that the ground was covered with petrified figures. Quickly he turned his back and, using his mirrored shield to guide him, began walking backward toward the hollow.

7   As Perseus neared the center of the hollow, he saw something moving in the reflection from his shield. It was the snakes on Medusa's head shimmering in the mirror. The serpents seemed relatively peaceful. Perseus guessed that Medusa was asleep. He hoped to slay her while she slept, but as he edged closer his foot accidentally kicked a stone. The stone clattered down into the hollow, and the monster awoke. Her mighty roar filled the air. Looking into his shield, Perseus could see her rise into view, her jaws agape and her terrible eyes flashing. With his back still turned, Perseus drew his sword. The creature hesitated for a moment, as if surprised that this man was not turning to stone. Then, snake heads hissing, Medusa rushed toward Perseus.

8   Perseus's heart pounded as the monster approached. He stood with his legs spread wide, braced for action. With one hand he held up his shield. In the other he gripped his sword. Soon Medusa was so close that Perseus could feel her hot breath on his neck. Still he stood his ground. He waited until her mouth was about to clamp down on him. Then he swept his sword around behind him in a slashing blow. He felt the cutting edge bite into Medusa's neck. There was a terrible cry. Then there was silence.

9   Perseus surveyed the dead monster's reflection. He did not turn to look at it with his own eyes. The gods had warned him that even in death Medusa's face would turn a person to stone. Carefully Perseus reached behind him and picked up the snake-covered head. He dropped it into a sack and began his return journey.

10   When Perseus arrived home, he found his mother in tears. She had been forced to agree to a marriage with King Polydectes. Perseus was furious. He went straight to the king's castle to confront him. When the king saw the young man, he was shocked. He had been sure that

Perseus would not return. As Polydectes watched, Perseus turned his head away and reached into his sack. Seeing that Perseus wasn't looking, the king grabbed a sword. Before he could strike, however, Perseus pulled the head of Medusa from the sack, and the king was instantly turned to stone.

11   Perseus became a hero in his kingdom. He had saved his mother from a marriage to a tyrant. He had freed the people from the rule of the evil Polydectes. And he had killed the fierce Medusa. 🍃

If you have been timed while reading this article, enter your reading time below. Then turn to the Words-per-Minute Table on page 71 and look up your reading speed (words per minute). Enter your reading speed on the graph on page 72.

Reading Time: **Lesson 3**

_____ : _____
Minutes   Seconds

A | Finding the Main Idea

One statement below expresses the main idea of the article. One statement is too general, or too broad. The other statement explains only part of the article; it is too narrow. Label the statements using the following key:

M—Main Idea   **B—Too Broad**   **N—Too Narrow**

_____ 1. Perseus, with the help of the gods, killed Medusa and saved his mother from the evil king Polydectes.

_____ 2. The evil king Polydectes tried to do away with Perseus by having him go after the terrible Medusa.

_____ 3. Perseus proved his courage when he fought with the monster Medusa.

_____ Score 15 points for a correct M answer.

_____ Score 5 points for each correct B or N answer.

_____ **Total Score:** Finding the Main Idea

B | Recalling Facts

How well do you remember the facts in the article? Put an X in the box next to the answer that correctly completes each statement about the article.

1. Polydectes told Perseus that slaying the monster would

☐ a. prevent the king's marriage to Perseus's mother.

☐ b. rid the kingdom of an evil force.

☐ c. prove Perseus's courage and manliness.

2. The hollow where Medusa lived was surrounded by

☐ a. stone figures of men.

☐ b. snakes.

☐ c. Greek gods.

3. Medusa was awakened by

☐ a. the writhing of the snakes on her head.

☐ b. a clattering stone.

☐ c. the reflection from Perseus's shiny shield.

4. When Perseus beheaded Medusa, she was

☐ a. above him.

☐ b. behind him.

☐ c. below him.

5. Perseus arrived home to find his mother

☐ a. married to Polydectes.

☐ b. dead of a broken heart.

☐ c. about to marry Polydectes.

Score 5 points for each correct answer.

_____ **Total Score:** Recalling Facts

C | Making Inferences

When you combine your own experience and information from a text to draw a conclusion that is not directly stated in that text, you are making an inference. Below are five statements that may or may not be inferences based on information in the article. Label the statements using the following key:

C—Correct Inference   **F—Faulty Inference**

_____ 1. Perseus was a god.

_____ 2. When Perseus set out to slay Medusa, he did not know that Polydectes wanted to marry his mother.

_____ 3. Without the help of the gods, Perseus could not have killed Medusa.

_____ 4. Medusa had no fear of any human.

_____ 5. When Perseus had killed Medusa, all those who had been turned to stone came back to life.

Score 5 points for each correct answer.

_____ **Total Score:** Making Inferences

D | Using Words Precisely

Each numbered sentence below contains an underlined word or phrase from the article. Following the sentence are three definitions. One definition is closest to the meaning of the underlined word. One definition is opposite or nearly opposite. Label those two definitions using the following key. Do not label the remaining definition.

C—Closest   **O—Opposite or Nearly Opposite**

1. He was <u>confident</u> that he had planned the perfect crime.

   _____ a. afraid

   _____ b. sure

   _____ c. uncertain

2. Although Perseus was nervous as he <u>contemplated</u> all of this, he did not want to seem like a coward.

   _____ a. asked about

   _____ b. ignored

   _____ c. studied

3. King Polydectes, a mythical ruler in ancient Greece, was <u>intensely</u> pleased with himself.

   _____ a. slightly

   _____ b. strongly

   _____ c. understandably

4. Looking into his shield, Perseus could see her rise into view, her jaws <u>agape</u> and her terrible eyes flashing.

   _____ a. wide open

   _____ b. bleeding

   _____ c. shut tight

5. In their <u>wrath</u>, they had turned her into a hideous monster.

_____ a. fear

_____ b. anger

_____ c. calm cheerfulness

_____ Score 3 points for each correct C answer.

_____ Score 2 points for each correct O answer.

_____ **Total Score:** Using Words Precisely

Enter the four total scores in the spaces below, and add them together to find your Reading Comprehension Score. Then record your score on the graph on page 73.

Score	Question Type	Lesson 3
_____	Finding the Main Idea	
_____	Recalling Facts	
_____	Making Inferences	
_____	Using Words Precisely	
_____	**Reading Comprehension Score**	

Author's Approach

Put an X in the box next to the correct answer.

1. The author uses the first paragraph of the article to

☐ a. tell the reader that the king is happy.

☐ b. describe the character of the king.

☐ c. compare the king and Perseus.

2. From the statements below, choose those that you believe the author would agree with.

☐ a. King Polydectes was popular with his people.

☐ b. Perseus was a brave young man.

☐ c. If Medusa had killed Perseus, Polydectes would have been responsible for the young man's death.

3. What does the author imply by saying "When at last he reached the hollow where the monster lived, Perseus saw that the ground was covered with petrified figures"?

☐ a. The petrified figures were men who had looked at Medusa and been turned to stone.

☐ b. The figures were men who had been badly frightened by Medusa.

☐ c. The ground was covered with the old bones of those who had tried to kill Medusa.

_____ Number of correct answers

Record your personal assessment of your work on the Critical Thinking Chart on page 74.

CRITICAL THINKING

Summarizing and Paraphrasing

Follow the directions provided for questions 1 and 2. Put an X in the box next to the correct answer for question 3.

1. Complete the following one-sentence summary of the article using the lettered phrases from the phrase bank below. Write the letters on the lines.

> **Phrase Bank:**
> a. Perseus's revenge on Polydectes
> b. how Perseus defeated and killed Medusa
> c. Polydectes's plan to kill Perseus

The article about Perseus and Medusa begins with _____, goes on to explain _____, and ends with _____.

2. Reread paragraph 1 in the article. Below, write a summary of the paragraph in no more than 25 words.

_____

_____

_____

_____

Reread your summary and decide whether it covers the important ideas in the paragraph. Next, decide how to shorten the summary to 15 words or less without leaving out any essential information. Write this summary below.

_____

_____

3. Choose the best one-sentence paraphrase for the following sentence from the article:
"Quickly he turned his back and, using his mirrored shield to guide him, began walking backward toward the hollow."

☐ a. Perseus turned around and walked back to the hollow.

☐ b. Perseus used his shield to protect himself as he walked back to the hollow.

☐ c. As Perseus walked backward in the direction of the hollow, he guided himself by looking at the reflection in the shield.

> _____ Number of correct answers
>
> Record your personal assessment of your work on the Critical Thinking Chart on page 74.

Critical Thinking

Put an X in the box next to the correct answer for questions 1 and 4. Follow the directions provided for questions 2 and 3.

1. From the information in paragraph 10, you can predict that

☐ a. King Polydectes would have stabbed Perseus to death if the young man hadn't pulled Medusa's head from his sack.

☐ b. Polydectes would have congratulated Perseus if the king had known that Medusa's head was in the sack.

☐ c. Perseus would have agreed to his mother's marriage if Polydectes had not sent him off to kill Medusa.

2. Choose from the letters below to correctly complete the following statement. Write the letters on the lines.

In the article, _____ and _____ are different.

   a. Medusa's effect on those who looked at her before she angered the gods

   b. Medusa's effect on those who looked at her when Perseus encountered her

   c. Medusa's effect on those who looked at her after she died

3. Think about cause-effect relationships in the article. Fill in the blanks in the cause-effect chart, drawing from the letters below.

Cause	Effect
_____	Medusa woke up.
Perseus pulled Medusa's head from his sack.	_____
Athena gave Perseus a mirrored shield.	_____

   a. He killed Medusa without having to look directly at her.

   b. Polydectes turned to stone.

   c. Perseus accidentally kicked a stone.

4. What did you have to do to answer question 2?

   ☐ a. find a cause (why something happened)

   ☐ b. find a contrast (how things are different)

   ☐ c. find an effect (something that happened)

_____ Number of correct answers

Record your personal assessment of your work on the Critical Thinking Chart on page 74.

Personal Response

Why do you think Perseus accepted the challenge to slay Medusa?

_____

_____

_____

_____

Self-Assessment

When reading the article, I was having trouble with

_____

_____

_____

_____

CRITICAL THINKING

BIGFOOT

Roger Patterson claimed to have taken this picture of Bigfoot, or Sasquatch, in 1967 using 16mm movie film.

He is known as Bigfoot. For years his very name has struck terror into the hearts of people on the Pacific Coast of North America. Hundreds claim to have seen him. Some know him by other names, such as Sasquatch, MoMo, or Skunk Ape. But all agree on what he looks like. He is reported to be between seven and nine feet tall, with large red eyes that glow in the dark. A sickening odor emanates from his hairy body. He has huge feet that make footprints measuring over 15 inches long.

2   Stories of Bigfoot have been around since the days of the early American Indians. Old Indian tales tell of wild men that were part animal. They were huge and hairy, with glowing eyes. According to the legends, they not only killed and ate cattle, but they also ate human beings.

3   There have been equally gruesome stories of Bigfoot in more recent times. One such story involves four gold miners. They built a cabin in a canyon near the volcano Mount St. Helens in Washington State. In 1924, they moved into the cabin and lived there peacefully until someone—

or something—began to rob their camp. When the miners looked for signs of the intruder, they discovered huge footprints in the dirt. Worried, the men began carrying guns.

4 One day soon after, the miners spied two apelike animals at the edge of a nearby cliff. Quickly the men raised their rifles and began shooting at the beasts. The bullets appeared to wound one animal, but it ran away. The second animal seemed to have been killed. All four men saw it plunge over the precipice. When they went to look for the body, however, they found nothing.

5 That night the men were awakened by a heavy pounding on the cabin roof and walls. Someone was throwing rocks at their cabin! The miners didn't dare go outside. They just stuck their rifles through cracks in the cabin walls and began firing. It was too dark to aim, but the men felt that they had to do something to protect themselves. When dawn arrived, the bombardment of rocks stopped. The miners stepped out and looked around. They saw rocks, blood, and enormous footprints all around the cabin.

6 It didn't take long for the miners' story to spread. As more and more people heard of the "apes" that had attacked the four

men, the canyon became known as Ape Valley. It is still known by that name.

7 The four gold miners were not the only ones to run into Bigfoot in 1924. A prospector working near Vancouver, British Columbia, also claimed to see the creature that season. In fact, he claimed that he had been kidnapped by a Bigfoot. The man said that he had been asleep in his sleeping bag when a Bigfoot appeared. The creature scooped up the sleeping bag, with the man in it, and slung it over his shoulder. For the next week, the prospector was held captive by a Bigfoot family. In addition to the one that captured him, he said, there were two other Bigfoot creatures. The three behaved as father, mother, and child.

8 During that week, the Bigfoot creatures seemed to be observing the man. He studied them, too. He concluded that they were not apes, but primitive human beings. They even talked to each other in a simple language.

9 The prospector finally managed to escape and find his way back to civilization. For a long time, he didn't tell anyone about his experience. Later, when asked why he remained silent, he claimed that he was afraid people would laugh at him. Supposedly, the man kept his secret for 33 years. As more and more Bigfoot

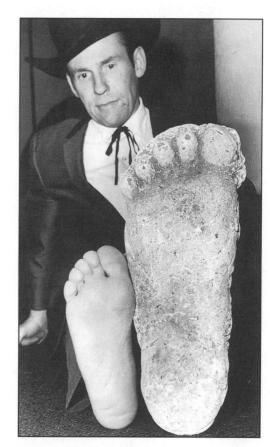

Photographer Roger Patterson claimed to have tracked Bigfoot through the forests near Eureka, California, in 1967. Here he compares his own foot to the cast he made of the footprint of Bigfoot.

sightings were reported, he decided to come forward with his story.

10   New Bigfoot sightings are still reported from time to time. No one knows exactly what a Bigfoot is or where it comes from. But several theories have been proposed. The most popular one is that Bigfoot is a primitive creature, half human and half ape. People who embrace this theory think that millions of years ago there were many such creatures. They believe that a few of their descendants are still around. At first it may seem that such creatures could not possibly have stayed so well hidden in today's crowded world. But there are still some great, dense forests in North America.

11   Another explanation is offered for Bigfoot's ability to avoid people. Some folks think that Bigfoot is a visitor from outer space. In this age of space adventure movies, it is not hard to imagine Bigfoot coming to Earth from another planet. In fact, whenever there is a Bigfoot sighting, there also seems to be an increase in the number of UFO sightings in the area.

12   Despite the many theories (some pretty farfetched), stories, and sightings of Bigfoot, we still have no proof that any such creature exists. Nobody has ever captured one. No Bigfoot bodies have ever been found. What we do have are many photographs of a beast that fits the descriptions, and many plaster casts of huge footprints. We also have a few feet of movie film showing a large hairy creature walking through the woods. The film was made by two men in a forest in northern California in 1967. One of the men had been a Bigfoot fan for years. He wanted to capture the creature on film. The men claim that they did find a Bigfoot. (At least they have some film of a hairy, upright creature.) In the film, the Bigfoot looks very much like a man walking around in a monster suit. Film experts and scientists who saw the movie couldn't tell whether this Bigfoot was real or a fake.

13   Is there a Bigfoot or isn't there? No one is sure. The photographs and plaster casts could be fakes. Or could they be real? Well, certainly the people in Skamamia,

Washington, seem convinced. There have been so many Bigfoot sightings around Skamamia that the town has passed a Bigfoot law. In Skamamia, it is illegal to kill a Bigfoot. Punishment for the crime is a fine of $10,000 and five years in jail. As yet, no one has been caught breaking that law. 🍃

If you have been timed while reading this article, enter your reading time below. Then turn to the Words-per-Minute Table on page 71 and look up your reading speed (words per minute). Enter your reading speed on the graph on page 72.

Reading Time: Lesson 4

_____ : _____

Minutes   Seconds

A **Finding the Main Idea**

One statement below expresses the main idea of the article. One statement is too general, or too broad. The other statement explains only part of the article; it is too narrow. Label the statements using the following key:

M—Main Idea   **B—Too Broad**   **N—Too Narrow**

_____ 1. Legends of a creature called Bigfoot have been widespread in North America for a very long time.

_____ 2. Although many people have claimed to have seen a Bigfoot, no bodies have ever been found.

_____ 3. Though there have been hundreds of reports of sightings of a large, hairy creature known as Bigfoot, there is no proof of Bigfoot's existence.

_____ Score 15 points for a correct M answer.

_____ Score 5 points for each correct B or N answer.

_____ **Total Score:** Finding the Main Idea

B **Recalling Facts**

How well do you remember the facts in the article? Put an X in the box next to the answer that correctly completes each statement about the article.

1. The miners who reported an encounter with a Bigfoot in 1924 were in
   ☐ a. California.
   ☐ b. Washington State.
   ☐ c. Skamamia.

2. The prospector captured by a Bigfoot
   ☐ a. hid from the creature in his sleeping bag.
   ☐ b. escaped by rolling up in a sleeping bag.
   ☐ c. was asleep in his sleeping bag when captured.

3. The prospector claimed that he delayed reporting his experience because he
   ☐ a. wanted to write a book about it.
   ☐ b. thought nobody would believe it.
   ☐ c. was afraid of the creatures.

4. No one has ever
   ☐ a. taken a picture of a Bigfoot.
   ☐ b. found a Bigfoot body.
   ☐ c. found Bigfoot footprints.

5. Skamamia, Washington,
   ☐ a. offers a reward of $10,000 for capturing a Bigfoot.
   ☐ b. offers $10,000 for a Bigfoot, dead or alive.
   ☐ c. has made it illegal to kill a Bigfoot.

Score 5 points for each correct answer.

_____ **Total Score:** Recalling Facts

C | Making Inferences

When you combine your own experience and information from a text to draw a conclusion that is not directly stated in that text, you are making an inference. Below are five statements that may or may not be inferences based on information in the article. Label the statements using the following key:

C—Correct Inference　　**F—Faulty Inference**

_____　1.　The Mount St. Helens miners were cautious men.

_____　2.　If there is such a creature as Bigfoot, it usually doesn't want anything to do with people.

_____　3.　The people of Skamamia, Washington, like the idea that Bigfoot may live near them.

_____　4.　Film experts concluded that the 1967 movie of Bigfoot was really a man in an ape suit.

_____　5.　The prospector was probably telling the truth about being held captive by a Bigfoot family because he had no reason to make up such a story.

Score 5 points for each correct answer.

_____ **Total Score:** Making Inferences

D | Using Words Precisely

Each numbered sentence below contains an underlined word or phrase from the article. Following the sentence are three definitions. One definition is closest to the meaning of the underlined word. One definition is opposite or nearly opposite. Label those two definitions using the following key. Do not label the remaining definition.

C—Closest　　**O—Opposite or Nearly Opposite**

1.　A sickening odor <u>emanates from</u> his hairy body.

_____　a.　is sprayed onto

_____　b.　goes into

_____　c.　comes from

2.　There have been equally <u>gruesome</u> stories of Bigfoot in more recent times.

_____　a.　horrible

_____　b.　pleasant

_____　c.　puzzling

3.　People who <u>embrace</u> this theory think that millions of years ago there were many such creatures, and that a few of their descendants are still around.

_____　a.　invent

_____　b.　accept

_____　c.　reject

4.　But there are still some great, <u>dense</u> forests in North America.

_____　a.　endangered

_____　b.　thick

_____　c.　sparse

5. Although no one knows exactly what a Bigfoot is or where it comes from, several theories have been <u>proposed</u>.

_____ a. put forward

_____ b. questioned

_____ c. held back

_____ Score 3 points for each correct C answer.

_____ Score 2 points for each correct O answer.

_____ **Total Score:** Using Words Precisely

Enter the four total scores in the spaces below, and add them together to find your Reading Comprehension Score. Then record your score on the graph on page 73.

Score	Question Type	Lesson 4
_____	Finding the Main Idea	
_____	Recalling Facts	
_____	Making Inferences	
_____	Using Words Precisely	
_____	**Reading Comprehension Score**	

Author's Approach

Put an X in the box next to the correct answer.

1. What does the author mean by the statement in paragraph 13 "As yet, no one has been caught breaking that law"?

☐ a. So far, there has been no evidence that anyone has killed a Bigfoot.

☐ b. So far, those who have killed a Bigfoot have not been caught.

☐ c. The people of Skamamia are very respectful of their town's laws.

2. What is the author's purpose in writing "Bigfoot"?

☐ a. To encourage the reader to believe that Bigfoot really exists

☐ b. To inform the reader about the intriguing possibility that Bigfoot exists

☐ c. To emphasize the similarities between a Bigfoot and a human

3. How is the author's purpose for writing the article expressed in paragraph 12?

☐ a. The author compares Bigfoot to a man walking around in a monster suit.

☐ b. The author describes a sighting during which witnesses supposedly filmed Bigfoot.

☐ c. The author points out that one of the men who claims to have filmed Bigfoot had been interested in Bigfoot for years.

4. The author tells this story mainly by

☐ a. telling the four gold miners' experience with Bigfoot.

☐ b. comparing Bigfoot sightings to UFO sightings.

☐ c. telling different stories about Bigfoot.

_____ Number of correct answers

Record your personal assessment of your work on the Critical Thinking Chart on page 74.

CRITICAL THINKING

Summarizing and Paraphrasing

Follow the directions provided for question 1. Put an X in the box next to the correct answer for question 2.

1. Look for the important ideas and events in paragraphs 7 and 8. Summarize those paragraphs in one or two sentences.

_____

_____

_____

2. Read the statement about the article below. Then read the paraphrase of that statement. Choose the reason that best tells why the paraphrase does not say the same thing as the statement.

Statement: Because there is an increase in UFO sightings whenever there is a Bigfoot sighting, some people believe that the big ape comes from outer space.

Paraphrase: Whenever there is a Bigfoot sighting, some people claim to have seen the ape alongside a UFO.

☐ a.   Paraphrase says too much.

☐ b.   Paraphrase doesn't say enough.

☐ c.   Paraphrase doesn't agree with the statement about the article.

_____

_____ Number of correct answers

Record your personal assessment of your work on the Critical Thinking Chart on page 74.

Critical Thinking

Follow the directions provided for questions 1, 3, and 5. Put an X in the box next to the correct answer for questions 2 and 4.

1. For each statement below, write O if it expresses an opinion and write F if it expresses a fact.

_____ a.   It is fun to think that millions of years ago, many primitive creatures that were half human and half ape roamed the earth.

_____ b.   States in the Northwest should pass laws protecting the Bigfoot.

_____ c.   In Skamamia, Washington, it is illegal to kill a Bigfoot.

2. From the article, you can predict that if someone killed a Bigfoot in Skamamia,

☐ a.   there would be no more Bigfoot sightings.

☐ b.   the person would be congratulated.

☐ c.   the person would be arrested for the crime.

3. Choose from the letters below to correctly complete the following statement. Write the letters on the lines.

In the article, _____ and _____ are alike.

a.   Sasquatch

b.   Skamamia

c.   MoMo

4. What was the cause of the four miners' decision to begin carrying guns?

☐ a. They wanted to kill and eat Bigfoot.

☐ b. They planned to rob other camps.

☐ c. They had been robbed, and they found huge footprints outside their cabin.

5. In which paragraph did you find the information or details to answer question 4?

_____

_____ Number of correct answers

Record your personal assessment of your work on the Critical Thinking Chart on page 74.

Self-Assessment

I was confused on question # _____ in section _____ because

_____

_____

_____

_____

Personal Response

Begin the first 5–8 sentences of your own article about a Bigfoot sighting. It may tell of a real experience or one that is imagined.

_____

_____

_____

_____

AMAZON SUPERSNAKE
The Giant Anaconda

Major Percy Fawcett had heard tales from local Indians of a giant snake living in the rivers of Brazil, but he didn't believe them. A surveyor for the Royal Geographic Society of London, Fawcett was skeptical of such legends. Then one day in 1907, he was drifting down the Rio Abuna. All at once, he saw the large triangular head of a snake near the bow of the boat. The tales *were* true, he thought to himself.

2   "It was a giant anaconda," Fawcett later claimed. Taking his rifle, he "smashed a .44 soft-nosed bullet into its spine, 10 feet below the wicked head." The wounded snake struggled to move the upper part of its body onto the riverbank. Its tail, though, still thrashed in the water around the canoe. Fawcett wrote: "We stepped ashore and approached the reptile with caution. It was out of action, but shivers ran up and down the body.... As far as it was possible to measure, a length of 45 feet lay out of the water, and 17 feet in it, making a total length of 62 feet."

3   Was this accurate? Could a snake really be that big? Fawcett was a credible witness. (He was the real-life inspiration

Major Percy Fawcett of the Royal Geographic Society (in one of the last photographs taken of him) had a difficult time convincing people that he had seen a snake that was 62 feet long.

for Steven Spielberg's Indiana Jones.) Still, hunters have often exaggerated the size of their prey. A 62-foot snake was too incredible for the experts at the Royal Geographic Society to believe. They ignored his report.

4   Fawcett could not drag the huge snake out of the jungle, so he could not prove his claim. From time to time, though, other people have seen even longer snakes. In the late 1940s, there were reports of another massive snake in Brazil. This creature was said to be between 60 and 150 feet long with glowing green eyes. Newspaper stories reported that it battled army soldiers and even knocked over buildings. But again, none of these wild tales was confirmed.

5   Today we know that the anaconda is real enough. And it is such a fierce creature that it is easy to see why people might exaggerate its true size and abilities. Padre Gumilla, a Jesuit priest, lived in Venezuela in the 1600s. He wrote that the anaconda could hypnotize its prey. The priest also claimed that the snake killed by shooting invisible poisonous vapors from its mouth. None of these claims is true. Still, the truth about the anaconda is scary enough. This is one animal you want to see only if it is behind a glass window at the zoo.

6   The anaconda is the world's largest snake. A few of the specimens that have

been found measure up to 40 feet long—about the length of a school bus. The anaconda's head has a prominent red stripe, and its olive-colored body has black markings. In the water, the snake is constantly flicking its menacing tongue. It uses its sense of taste to discover what is going on around it. The anaconda is also the heaviest snake—especially after it eats.

This 19-foot, 90-pound anaconda is small compared to some of the giant specimens that have been found.

One female anaconda weighed in at 500 pounds.

7   The giant anaconda is a kind of boa constrictor. To kill, it sinks its teeth into an animal. It then wraps itself around the prey. The snake literally squeezes, or constricts, the prey into submission. Next, the snake takes its poor victim under-water. There it swallows the animal whole. Unfortunately, the victim is often still alive and might remain so for hours in the beast's stomach!

8   It may take up to a week for the snake to fully digest its meal. During this time, it spends its time basking in the sun by a riverbank. When the snake doesn't have a full stomach, though, it is extremely dangerous. If you ever go camping in the Amazon, take care. It would be most unwise to go for a swim in the river after dark. The anaconda can sneak up on its prey with great cunning, barely rippling the water. And the snake can swim much faster than humans. That is why the anaconda is so feared by the native people of the region. These jungle residents regard the monster as one of the seven "curses" of the Amazon.

9   Most of the time the anaconda feeds on fish, birds, crocodiles, turtles, and deer. Early Spanish settlers called the snake *matatoro*, or "bull killer." There is no proof that an anaconda ever really ate a bull, but it is possible. Like most snakes, it can unhinge its jaw. That allows it to swallow an animal larger than itself.

10   Attacks on humans are rare. But once in a great while they do occur. In April 1977, an attack took place in a remote region of Peru. An 18-foot anaconda killed three children aged 7, 11, and 13. The children had been fishing on a boat. Witnesses said that a big snake toppled the boat and then crushed the children.

11   Despite its size, little is known about the anaconda. The snake spends most of its time in murky rivers with just its head above the surface. Shy by nature, it seldom emerges from the water long enough to be seen. And it inhabits a part of the world where very few people live. So when it does leave the water, there may be no one around to see it. Few attempts have been made to study the snake in its natural habitat. Even the experts can't agree on how large this snake might grow. It's quite possible that the largest specimens have not been found yet. ❧

If you have been timed while reading this article, enter your reading time below. Then turn to the Words-per-Minute Table on page 71 and look up your reading speed (words per minute). Enter your reading speed on the graph on page 72.

Reading Time: Lesson 5

_____ : _____

Minutes   *Seconds*

A | Finding the Main Idea

One statement below expresses the main idea of the article. One statement is too general, or too broad. The other statement explains only part of the article; it is too narrow. Label the statements using the following key:

M—Main Idea   **B—Too Broad**   **N—Too Narrow**

_____ 1. When Major Percy Fawcett reported that he had seen a 62-foot snake, the Royal Geographic Society didn't believe him.

_____ 2. The anaconda is one of the most fascinating animals in the world.

_____ 3. The giant anaconda, the world's largest snake, is a kind of boa constrictor about which little is known.

_____ Score 15 points for a correct M answer.

_____ Score 5 points for each correct B or N answer.

_____ **Total Score:** Finding the Main Idea

B | Recalling Facts

How well do you remember the facts in the article? Put an X in the box next to the answer that correctly completes each statement about the article.

1. Major Percy Fawcett was a surveyor for
   - ☐ a.   Steven Spielberg.
   - ☐ b.   the Royal Geographic Society.
   - ☐ c.   Padre Gumilla.

2. To discover what is going on around it, the anaconda uses
   - ☐ a.   its sense of smell.
   - ☐ b.   invisible poisonous vapors.
   - ☐ c.   its sense of taste.

3. After the anaconda sinks its teeth into an animal, it
   - ☐ a.   bites its head off.
   - ☐ b.   wraps around and squeezes its prey.
   - ☐ c.   drags it up onto the riverbank.

4. The native people of the Amazon jungle regard the anaconda as
   - ☐ a.   harmless and shy.
   - ☐ b.   *matatoro,* or "bull killer."
   - ☐ c.   one of the seven curses of the Amazon.

5. The anaconda spends most of its time
   - ☐ a.   in trees.
   - ☐ b.   on land.
   - ☐ c.   in rivers.

Score 5 points for each correct answer.

_____ **Total Score:** Recalling Facts

C | Making Inferences

When you combine your own experience and information from a text to draw a conclusion that is not directly stated in that text, you are making an inference. Below are five statements that may or may not be inferences based on information in the article. Label the statements using the following key:

C—Correct Inference   F—Faulty Inference

_____ 1. The anaconda poses a great threat to human life around the world.

_____ 2. Major Percy Fawcett led an adventurous life.

_____ 3. Padre Gumilla purposely fooled people with his inaccurate stories about the anaconda.

_____ 4. Scientists have made few attempts to study anacondas because they feel that these snakes are simply not very interesting.

_____ 5. As a general rule, most people should avoid swimming in the Amazon River.

Score 5 points for each correct answer.

_____ **Total Score:** Making Inferences

D | Using Words Precisely

Each numbered sentence below contains an underlined word or phrase from the article. Following the sentence are three definitions. One definition is closest to the meaning of the underlined word. One definition is opposite or nearly opposite. Label those two definitions using the following key. Do not label the remaining definition.

C—Closest   O—Opposite or Nearly Opposite

1. Its tail, though, still <u>thrashed</u> in the water around the canoe.

_____ a. lashed out

_____ b. was visible

_____ c. lay still

2. Still, hunters have often <u>exaggerated</u> the size of their prey.

_____ a. underrated

_____ b. recorded

_____ c. overstated

3. The snake literally squeezes, or constricts, the prey into <u>submission</u>.

_____ a. attack mode

_____ b. a state of surrender

_____ c. unconsciousness

4. The anaconda can sneak up on its prey with great <u>cunning</u>, barely rippling the water.

_____ a. silence

_____ b. dullness

_____ c. slyness

5. The snake spends most of its time in <u>murky</u> rivers with just its head above the surface.

_____ a. dark

_____ b. warm

_____ c. clear

_____ Score 3 points for each correct C answer.

_____ Score 2 points for each correct O answer.

_____ **Total Score:** Using Words Precisely

Enter the four total scores in the spaces below, and add them together to find your Reading Comprehension Score. Then record your score on the graph on page 73.

Score	Question Type	Lesson 5
_____	Finding the Main Idea	
_____	Recalling Facts	
_____	Making Inferences	
_____	Using Words Precisely	
_____	**Reading Comprehension Score**	

Author's Approach

Put an X in the box next to the correct answer.

1. What does the author mean by the statement "Fawcett was a credible witness"?

☐ a. Fawcett could not be trusted.

☐ b. Fawcett could be counted on to report what he saw accurately.

☐ c. Fawcett frequently gave evidence in legal trials.

2. The main purpose of the first paragraph is to

☐ a. inform the reader about the Royal Geographic Society.

☐ b. entertain the reader with an adventure story.

☐ c. introduce the reader to the possibility that a giant snake exists.

3. Choose the statement below that best describes the author's position in paragraph 8.

☐ a. The anaconda is particularly dangerous in the water.

☐ b. No one should ever go camping in the Amazon area.

☐ c. The native people of the Amazon do not respect the giant anaconda.

4. The author probably wrote this article in order to

☐ a. tell the reader about Major Fawcett.

☐ b. describe the qualities of the giant anaconda.

☐ c. convince the reader that the giant anaconda should be wiped out.

_____ Number of correct answers

Record your personal assessment of your work on the Critical Thinking Chart on page 74.

Summarizing and Paraphrasing

Follow the directions provided for question 1. Put an X in the box next to the correct answer for question 2.

1. Reread paragraph 10 in the article. Below, write a summary of the paragraph in no more than 25 words.

_____

_____

_____

Reread your summary and decide whether it covers the important ideas in the paragraph. Next, decide how to shorten the summary to 15 words or less without leaving out any essential information. Write this summary below.

_____

_____

_____

2. Read the statement about the article below. Then read the paraphrase of that statement. Choose the reason that best tells why the paraphrase does not say the same thing as the statement.

Statement: In the 1940s, newspaper stories reported that a snake 60 to 150 feet long with glowing green eyes had fought against army soldiers and knocked over buildings in Brazil.

Paraphrase: In the 1940s, soldiers told newspaper reporters in Brazil that they had seen a huge snake with shiny green eyes destroy some buildings.

☐ a. Paraphrase says too much.

☐ b. Paraphrase doesn't say enough.

☐ c. Paraphrase doesn't agree with the statement about the article.

_____ Number of correct answers

Record your personal assessment of your work on the Critical Thinking Chart on page 74.

Critical Thinking

Follow the directions provided for questions 1, 3, and 4. Put an X in the box next to the correct answer for the other questions.

1. For each statement below, write O if it expresses an opinion and write F if it expresses a fact.

_____ a. The anaconda is the world's largest and heaviest snake.

_____ b. Major Fawcett was the inspiration for Indiana Jones.

_____ c. The anaconda is the greatest curse of the Amazon.

2. From the article, you can predict that if Major Fawcett hadn't shot the anaconda, the snake might have

  ☐ a. overturned Fawcett's boat and crushed him.

  ☐ b. swallowed the boat.

  ☐ c. shot poisonous vapors from its mouth.

3. Choose from the letters below to correctly complete the following statement. Write the letters on the lines.

  On the positive side, _____, but on the negative side _____.

  a. an anaconda attacked three young children in 1977

  b. anacondas are fascinating and impressive creatures

  c. no one knows how large the snakes might grow

4. Reread paragraph 3. Then choose from the letters below to correctly complete the following statement. Write the letters on the lines.

  According to paragraph 3, _____ because _____.

  a. experts at the Royal Geographic Society ignored Fawcett's report

  b. Fawcett was a credible witness

  c. they thought Fawcett was exaggerating the size of the anaconda

5. What did you have to do to answer question 2?

  ☐ a. find an opinion (what someone thinks about something)

  ☐ b. find a cause (why something happened)

  ☐ c. make a prediction (what might happen next)

_____ Number of correct answers

Record your personal assessment of your work on the Critical Thinking Chart on page 74.

Personal Response

What was most surprising or interesting to you about this article?

_____

_____

_____

_____

Self-Assessment

From reading this article, I have learned

_____

_____

_____

_____

CRITICAL THINKING

THE JERSEY DEVIL

May the devil take this one!"

2   That, according to one legend, is what Mrs. Leeds said before she gave birth to her 13th child. The year was 1735. Mrs. Leeds lived in poverty with her 12 starving children in the Pine Barrens region of southeastern New Jersey. Apparently, someone heard her plea. Legend has it that the baby crawled from the womb terribly deformed. It had the head of a collie, the wings of a bat, and cloven feet. Quickly it flew out the window and into the woods. Since then the monster, known as the Jersey Devil, has been haunting the Pine Barrens.

3   That, however, is just the most popular version of the story. There are many others. According to some accounts, the mother's name was Mrs. Shrouds and she lived in Leeds Point, New Jersey. One tale claims that the child was born deformed, but the mother tried to protect it from public ridicule. Then on a stormy night, the child flapped its arms, turning them

This drawing shows the winged creature with the head of a horse that Mr. and Mrs. Nelson Evans claimed to have seen on a shed roof in Gloucester, New Jersey, in 1909. Had they seen the Jersey Devil?

into bat wings. The child then disappeared up the chimney. Still another story suggests that the child was not born deformed at all and only later turned into a hideous creature. Even the Jersey Devil's year of birth isn't certain. At least five different years have been suggested.

4   Whatever its true origin, the story of the Jersey Devil seems to be indestructible. And it keeps popping up again and again. In the early 1800s, naval hero Stephen Decatur saw the Jersey Devil flying across the sky. Decatur was testing cannonballs at the time. He fired and hit the creature, but it kept going in spite of the hole in its body. Joseph Bonaparte, the brother of Napoleon, claimed he saw the Jersey Devil while hunting in New Jersey. Others found strange tracks and heard odd screams at night. Fear became so intense in some parts of the Pine Barrens that locals refused to leave their homes after dark.

5   With the dawn of the 20th century, reports of the Jersey Devil died out for a time. Charles Skinner, an expert on American myths, declared that the days of the Jersey Devil were gone for good. Perhaps the creature was dead. Or perhaps people had just stopped believing in it. Either way, the people in the Pine Barrens could now go about their daily lives without fear.

6   Then, with no warning, the fear came rushing back. Once more, thousands of people began seeing the Jersey Devil. The creature was observed all over the state. Sightings occurred from the seacoast to Pennsylvania. By January 16, 1909, people had begun to panic. Zack Cozzens from Woodbury, New Jersey, saw a flying creature. "I first heard a hissing sound," he reported. "Then something white flew across the street." The monster had glowing green eyes and flew "as fast as an auto." Another man saw the same monster perched on the edge of a canal. Police officers shot at it but couldn't seem to hit it.

7   Meanwhile, bizarre footprints were turning up all over the place. That was especially true in Burlington, New Jersey. The prints went from roof to roof. They went down streets and then just disappeared in the middle of the road. Sometimes they stopped in the middle of a field as if made by a bird that had taken flight. No one could identify the prints. Two animal trappers said they had never seen tracks like those. Most people believed that the footprints belonged to the Jersey Devil.

8   On January 19th, the Jersey Devil paid a call on Mr. and Mrs. Nelson Evans of Gloucester. The monster arrived at 2:30 A.M. and began making weird noises. The couple looked out the window. They spotted the creature dancing on the roof of a woodshed. "It was about three and a half feet high, with a head like a collie dog and a face like a horse," said Mr. Evans.

The Jersey Devil has become a part of local folklore, even making its way onto souvenir postcards such as this.

The Jersey Devil kept howling and dancing for 10 minutes. "My wife and I were scared, I tell you," said Mr. Evans. "But I managed to open the window and say, 'Shoo,' and it...flew away."

9   The sightings, which lasted until January 23rd, caused a sensation. They made front page news in Philadelphia. The story was also reported in the papers in other parts of the country. Most dismissed it as a joke. One newspaper editor said that the Jersey Devil was just a product of the imagination of "complete idiots." The Philadelphia Zoo also joined the fun. Zoo officials offered a $10,000 reward for the capture of the Jersey Devil. Norman Jeffries and Jacob F. Hope dressed up a kangaroo in green paint, feathers, and antlers. They put the "creature" on display and charged the public a fee to see it.

10   Eventually, the Jersey Devil dropped out of sight. The creature wasn't seen again until 1927. Then a taxi driver saw it while changing a flat tire. The Jersey Devil jumped onto the roof of the man's cab and shook the vehicle violently before flying off. In 1951, it was spotted again. A 10-year-old boy claimed seeing a creature "with blood dripping from its face." After that, many other people reported sighting the Jersey Devil. Again strange tracks were found—but this time police determined they had been made by a stuffed bear paw attached to a stick. The police were not amused. They began posting signs along highways that read "The Jersey Devil Is a Hoax." Still, some people didn't believe the police. They organized hunting parties, hoping to kill the Jersey Devil. Of course, the police didn't approve of people running around with guns, endangering their lives and those of others. As a result, the police arrested several "Devil hunters."

11   Once again the hysteria died down. Since then, the Jersey Devil has spent most of its time in hiding. But every once in a while it pops out again. In 1966, for instance, a farmer claimed that the Jersey Devil had killed all his livestock. Eight years later, an ambulance driver claimed he heard the Jersey Devil screaming in the woods. And so it goes.

12   Although the creature is quite elusive these days, there is still one certain way to see a Jersey Devil—or several of them for that matter. The National Hockey League team from New Jersey is known as the New Jersey Devils.

If you have been timed while reading this article, enter your reading time below. Then turn to the Words-per-Minute Table on page 71 and look up your reading speed (words per minute). Enter your reading speed on the graph on page 72.

Reading Time: Lesson 6

_____ : _____

Minutes   Seconds

A Finding the Main Idea

One statement below expresses the main idea of the article. One statement is too general, or too broad. The other statement explains only part of the article; it is too narrow. Label the statements using the following key:

M—Main Idea   **B—Too Broad**   **N—Too Narrow**

_____ 1. There are many stories about the origin of the Jersey Devil.

_____ 2. Since the 1700s, people have reported seeing a winged creature known as the Jersey Devil flying throughout parts of the Northeast.

_____ 3. In 1909, one couple saw the Jersey Devil howling and dancing on the roof of a woodshed.

_____ Score 15 points for a correct M answer.

_____ Score 5 points for each correct B or N answer.

_____ **Total Score:** Finding the Main Idea

B Recalling Facts

How well do you remember the facts in the article? Put an X in the box next to the answer that correctly completes each statement about the article.

1. According to a popular legend, when Mrs. Leeds gave birth to her 13th child, the baby
   ☐ a. crawled from the womb terribly deformed.
   ☐ b. turned into a hideous creature later on.
   ☐ c. flapped its arms, turning them into bat wings.

2. The naval hero who fired and hit the Jersey Devil with a cannonball was
   ☐ a. Charles Skinner.
   ☐ b. Joseph Bonaparte.
   ☐ c. Stephen Decatur.

3. On January 19th, 1909, Mr. and Mrs. Evans saw the Jersey Devil
   ☐ a. on the roof of a cab.
   ☐ b. on the roof of a woodshed.
   ☐ c. with blood dripping from its face.

4. After the Jersey Devil made front page news in 1909, officials at the Philadelphia Zoo
   ☐ a. dressed up a kangaroo and put it on public display.
   ☐ b. dismissed the sightings as a joke.
   ☐ c. offered a reward for the creature's capture.

5. The New Jersey Devils is the name of a
   ☐ a. National Hockey League team.
   ☐ b. Jersey Devil hunting party.
   ☐ c. National Basketball Association team.

Score 5 points for each correct answer.

_____ **Total Score:** Recalling Facts

C | Making Inferences

When you combine your own experience and information from a text to draw a conclusion that is not directly stated in that text, you are making an inference. Below are five statements that may or may not be inferences based on information in the article. Label the statements using the following key:

C—Correct Inference   **F—Faulty Inference**

_____ 1. The people who made the Jersey Devil tracks using a stuffed bear paw attached to a stick were trying to fool others.

_____ 2. In 1909, some people hoped to make a profit from the Jersey Devil scare.

_____ 3. The police in areas where the Jersey Devil was sighted were amused by the creature.

_____ 4. The Jersey Devil apparently cannot be killed.

_____ 5. Everyone in New Jersey believes in the Jersey Devil.

> Score 5 points for each correct answer.
>
> _____ **Total Score:** Making Inferences

D | Using Words Precisely

Each numbered sentence below contains an underlined word or phrase from the article. Following the sentence are three definitions. One definition is closest to the meaning of the underlined word. One definition is opposite or nearly opposite. Label those two definitions using the following key. Do not label the remaining definition.

C—Closest   **O—Opposite or Nearly Opposite**

1. Legend has it that the baby crawled from the womb terribly underlined deformed.

_____ a. slowly

_____ b. disfigured

_____ c. well-built

2. One tale claims that the child was born deformed, but the mother tried to protect it from public ridicule.

_____ a. approval

_____ b. places

_____ c. taunting

3. Still another story suggests that the child was not born deformed at all and only later turned into a hideous creature.

_____ a. horrifying

_____ b. shy

_____ c. lovely

4. Once again the hysteria died down.

_____ a. extreme happiness

_____ b. extreme calm

_____ c. extreme excitement

5. Although the creature is quite <u>elusive</u> these days, there is still one certain way to see a Jersey Devil—or several of them for that matter.

_____ a. hard to find

_____ b. easy to observe

_____ c. dangerous

_____ Score 3 points for each correct C answer.

_____ Score 2 points for each correct O answer.

_____ **Total Score:** Using Words Precisely

Enter the four total scores in the spaces below, and add them together to find your Reading Comprehension Score. Then record your score on the graph on page 73.

Score	Question Type	Lesson 6
_____	Finding the Main Idea	
_____	Recalling Facts	
_____	Making Inferences	
_____	Using Words Precisely	
_____	**Reading Comprehension Score**	

Author's Approach

Put an X in the box next to the correct answer.

1. The author uses the first sentence of the article to
   - ☐ a. engage the reader's interest.
   - ☐ b. describe the qualities of the Jersey Devil.
   - ☐ c. inform the reader about Mrs. Leeds and her relationship to her children.

2. What does the author imply by saying "Fear became so intense in some parts of the Pine Barrens that locals refused to leave their homes after dark"?
   - ☐ a. People in the Pine Barrens region had become panic-stricken over the Jersey Devil sightings.
   - ☐ b. People in the Pine Barrens region were angered by the Jersey Devil sightings.
   - ☐ c. Most people in the Pine Barrens region didn't believe in the Jersey Devil.

3. The author tells this story mainly by
   - ☐ a. telling one person's experience with the Jersey Devil.
   - ☐ b. comparing the Jersey Devil to other monsters sighted around New Jersey.
   - ☐ c. telling different stories about the Jersey Devil.

_____ Number of correct answers

Record your personal assessment of your work on the Critical Thinking Chart on page 74.

CRITICAL THINKING

Summarizing and Paraphrasing

Follow the directions provided for questions 1 and 2. Put an X in the box next to the correct answer for question 3.

1. Look for the important ideas and events in paragraphs 6 and 7. Summarize those paragraphs in one or two sentences.

_____

_____

_____

2. Complete the following one-sentence summary of the article using the lettered phrases from the phrase bank below. Write the letters on the lines.

> **Phrase Bank:**
> a. how people have reacted to sightings of the creature over the years
> b. one sure way to see a Jersey Devil
> c. stories about the creature's origin

The article about the Jersey Devil begins with _____, goes on to explain _____, and ends with _____.

3. Choose the best one-sentence paraphrase for the following sentence from the article:
"Of course, the police didn't approve of people running around with guns, endangering their lives and those of others."

☐ a. The people carrying guns put the police in danger.

☐ b. The police were afraid that the people carrying guns might hurt themselves or others.

☐ c. The police risked other people's lives by carrying guns.

> _____ Number of correct answers
>
> Record your personal assessment of your work on the Critical Thinking Chart on page 74.

Critical Thinking

Put an X in the box next to the correct answer for questions 1, 2, and 4. Follow the directions provided for the other questions.

1. Which of the following statements from the article is an opinion rather than a fact?

☐ a. "Zoo officials offered a $10,000 reward for the capture of the Jersey Devil."

☐ b. "The National Hockey League team from New Jersey is known as the New Jersey Devils."

☐ c. "The Jersey Devil was just a product of the imagination of 'complete idiots.'"

2. From the information in paragraph 11, you can predict that

☐ a. no one will ever see the Jersey Devil again.

☐ b. the Jersey Devil will become a threat to all livestock in New Jersey.

☐ c. people will continue to report seeing the Jersey Devil.

3. Choose from the letters below to correctly complete the following statement. Write the letters on the lines.

In the article, _____ and _____ are alike.

a. the description of Mrs. Leeds's 13th child

b. the description of the creature displayed by Norman Jeffries and Jacob F. Hope

c. Mr. Evans's description of the Jersey Devil

4. What was the effect of the Jersey Devil sightings in January 1909?

☐ a. People went about their daily life without fear.

☐ b. Many people panicked.

☐ c. The Jersey Devil flew "as fast as an auto."

5. In which paragraph did you find the information or details to answer question 4?

_____

_____ Number of correct answers

Record your personal assessment of your work on the Critical Thinking Chart on page 74.

Personal Response

Would you recommend this article to other students? Explain.

_____

_____

_____

_____

Self-Assessment

While reading the article, I found it easiest to

_____

_____

_____

_____

FABULOUS FAKES
Monster Hoaxes

The two workmen had been digging for hours under the hot autumn sun. Although digging a well was hard work, the job had been going smoothly. The workers were pleased with the progress they were making. Suddenly, though, they heard a sharp "Clang!" One of the shovels had struck something. At first the men thought they had hit a rock. As they started to dig around the object, however, they found that it had a strange shape. Growing anxious about what they would find, they began to dig frantically. Soon they unearthed a foot, then a leg, then the rest of a body. It was a man. But what a man! He was 10 feet, four and a half inches tall, and he was made entirely of stone!

2   The well diggers were astonished. They knew that according to the Bible there had once been giants on the earth. So they thought it was logical that the remains of those giants should lie somewhere in the earth. But they were amazed to think that they had found the first body there on a New York farm in the mid-1800s.

Even after it was declared a hoax, the Cardiff Giant captured people's imaginations. Here, the stone giant is displayed in New York in the 1940s.

3   As they stared at the stone man, the workmen grew more and more excited. They were sure that they would become famous. After all, they had just made one of the greatest scientific discoveries of the 19th century. Surely this giant fossil was the most important find in the history of paleontology!

4   There was only one thing wrong with the workmen's discovery: the stone giant was one of the biggest frauds of all time.

5   The stone giant was actually the creation of a man named George Hull. Hull, who made cigars from the tobacco he grew on his farm, lived in Binghamton, New York. He had dreamed up the idea of a stone giant while visiting his sister. During the visit, he had gone to church. The preacher spoke about the giants mentioned in the Bible. From the sermon, Hull got the notion of burying a stone man and then promoting it as a petrified Biblical giant.

6   Hull convinced his business partner, H. B. Martin, to help him with the hoax. First the two men obtained a five-ton block of gypsum. Then they hired two sculptors to carve the statue. Hull was the model for the figure. It took the sculptors three months of hard work to finish the job. When they were through, Hull began his own work on the statue. Using a darning needle, he pounded thousands of tiny holes into the soft stone. This made the giant's skin look like it had pores. Then Hull "aged" the giant figure by pouring sulfuric acid all over it.

7   The completed giant was crated and shipped by rail to a train station near a farm in Cardiff, New York. When it arrived there, Hull had the crate placed in a wagon. It took four horses to pull the heavy load to the farm in Cardiff. Once Hull had the stone man on the farm, he buried it. He let a year pass. Then he hired the unsuspecting workmen to dig a well in the spot where the giant was buried.

8   Newspapers hailed the giant as the Eighth Wonder of the World. They called it the "American Goliath." Hull placed the giant on display in a tent and charged 50 cents admission to view it. In those days, 50 cents was a full day's pay for the average worker. Despite the high price, as many as 500 people paid to see the giant every weekday. One Sunday, more than 2,000 people paid it a visit.

9   Hull was anxious to sell the statue before it was revealed as a fake. He soon sold three-quarters of his rights to some businessmen. They moved the figure to nearby Syracuse. The new partners thought that the giant would draw an even bigger crowd in that large city, and they were right. Thousands viewed the figure and went away marveling over it.

But O. C. Marsh, a young paleontologist from Yale University, took one look at the giant and declared it a "decided humbug."

10   At that point, George Hull confessed to the entire hoax. But even though the whole world then knew it to be a fake, people kept going to see the giant. The

The Cardiff Giant was 10 feet long and made of gypsum stone.

great showman P. T. Barnum had a copy of the statue made, and he put it on exhibit in his museum. People even flocked there to see what they knew to be a copy of a fake. Today, George Hull's giant still draws crowds. The Cardiff Giant, as it came to be called, is one of the exhibits at the museum of the New York State Historical Association in Cooperstown.

11   Are you amazed that people could be tricked into believing that Hull's stone statue was really the body of a giant? Then you will be truly astonished at the fakes known as "fur-bearing trout." Mounted specimens are sometimes exhibited at fairs. They can also be found in bars in Canada and across the northern United States. The people who display them explain that the unusual fish live only in deep water that is very cold. The fish adapted to their icy environment by growing fur for warmth. The deeper the water in which the fish are caught, the tricksters will tell you, the thicker their fur.

12   The truth is that taxidermists attached the fur to the bodies of dead trout. And though the furry trout look realistic, it is surprising that people believe the far-fetched stories about them.

13   Another outlandish creature is the "jackalope." This animal looks like a rabbit with antlers. It is said to be a rare species that is in danger of dying out. Like the fur-bearing trout, however, the antlered rabbit is a fake. It is made by attaching the antlers of an antelope to the body of a jackrabbit. Hence its name.

14   One other creature that has been the object of many hoaxes is the mermaid. Over the course of many centuries, sailors reported seeing mermaids frolicking in the open seas. Many of those seagoing men truly believed that they had seen ocean creatures with the heads and torsos of women and the lower bodies of fish. Eventually, some crooked taxidermists who knew how gullible people could be decided to cash in on the legends. They made up their own mermaid specimens and exhibited them for a fee. Historically, mermaids have been reported to be beautiful creatures about the size of women. The fake mermaids, however, were small and grotesque. That was because most of them were made up of the head, shoulders, and chest of a shaved monkey joined to the body and tail of a fish. Other mermaid fakes were made by stitching the head and shoulders of an ape

to the tail of a porpoise. Those "mermaids" were larger, but no less ugly.

15   It is almost unbelievable that people would fall for such outrageous fakes as the monkey mermaids, stone giant, fur-bearing trout, and jackalope. But our imaginations can reach far beyond the world we live in. What we can imagine is often more exciting and interesting than the routine of our daily lives. The fakes provided food for people's imaginations. 🍃

If you have been timed while reading this article, enter your reading time below. Then turn to the Words-per-Minute Table on page 71 and look up your reading speed (words per minute). Enter your reading speed on the graph on page 72.

Reading Time: Lesson 7

_____ : _____

Minutes   Seconds

A | Finding the Main Idea

One statement below expresses the main idea of the article. One statement is too general, or too broad. The other statement explains only part of the article; it is too narrow. Label the statements using the following key:

M—Main Idea   **B—Too Broad**   **N—Too Narrow**

_____ 1. The Cardiff Giant was a successful hoax that continues to attract attention.

_____ 2. Over the years, many people have been fooled into believing that various fake creatures were real.

_____ 3. There have always been a great number of people gullible enough to be fooled into believing outlandish things.

_____ Score 15 points for a correct M answer.

_____ Score 5 points for each correct B or N answer.

_____ **Total Score:** Finding the Main Idea

B | Recalling Facts

How well do you remember the facts in the article? Put an X in the box next to the answer that correctly completes each statement about the article.

1. Hull got the idea for making a stone giant from
   - ☐ a. reading his Bible.
   - ☐ b. listening to a preacher.
   - ☐ c. his business partner.

2. The model for the Cardiff Giant was
   - ☐ a. Hull.
   - ☐ b. Hull's sister.
   - ☐ c. Hull's partner.

3. The Cardiff Giant was carved by
   - ☐ a. Hull.
   - ☐ b. two well diggers.
   - ☐ c. two sculptors.

4. Specimens of fur-bearing trout can be found
   - ☐ a. in both Binghamton and Syracuse, New York.
   - ☐ b. in the northern United States and Canada.
   - ☐ c. at a museum of the New York State Historical Association.

5. A jackalope is made by combining
   - ☐ a. a jackrabbit and an antelope.
   - ☐ b. a monkey and a fish.
   - ☐ c. an ape and a porpoise.

Score 5 points for each correct answer.

_____ **Total Score:** Recalling Facts

C | Making Inferences

When you combine your own experience and information from a text to draw a conclusion that is not directly stated in that text, you are making an inference. Below are five statements that may or may not be inferences based on information in the article. Label the statements using the following key:

C—Correct Inference   **F—Faulty Inference**

_____ 1. The sculptors who carved the Cardiff Giant agreed to keep George Hull's secret.

_____ 2. Fur-bearing trout really may exist in some unexplored areas of the ocean.

_____ 3. To be believable, fur-bearing trout and jackalopes are made with great care.

_____ 4. The fact that the Cardiff Giant was proved false means that there never were giants on the earth.

_____ 5. People today could not be fooled by fake creatures.

Score 5 points for each correct answer.

_____ **Total Score:** Making Inferences

D | Using Words Precisely

Each numbered sentence below contains an underlined word or phrase from the article. Following the sentence are three definitions. One definition is closest to the meaning of the underlined word. One definition is opposite or nearly opposite. Label those two definitions using the following key. Do not label the remaining definition.

C—Closest   **O—Opposite or Nearly Opposite**

1. George Hull, who made cigars from the tobacco he grew on his farm in Binghamton, New York, had dreamed up the whole <u>hoax</u>.

_____ a. deceitful act

_____ b. honest act

_____ c. final act

2. Newspapers <u>hailed</u> the giant as the Eighth Wonder of the World.

_____ a. praised

_____ b. summarized

_____ c. condemned

3. But O. C. Marsh took one look at the giant and declared it a "decided <u>humbug</u>."

_____ a. pest

_____ b. fraud

_____ c. real thing

4. Then Hull "<u>aged</u>" the giant figure by pouring sulfuric acid all over it.

_____ a. made it look newer

_____ b. determined the age of

_____ c. made it look older

5. Eventually, some crooked taxidermists who knew how <u>gullible</u> people could be, decided to cash in on the legends.

_____ a. suspicious

_____ b. easy to fool

_____ c. fortunate

_____ Score 3 points for each correct C answer.

_____ Score 2 points for each correct O answer.

_____ **Total Score:** Using Words Precisely

Enter the four total scores in the spaces below, and add them together to find your Reading Comprehension Score. Then record your score on the graph on page 73.

Score	Question Type	Lesson 7
_____	Finding the Main Idea	
_____	Recalling Facts	
_____	Making Inferences	
_____	Using Words Precisely	
_____	**Reading Comprehension Score**	

Author's Approach

Put an X in the box next to the correct answer.

1. The main purpose of the first paragraph is to
   - ☐ a. describe the workmen's amazing discovery.
   - ☐ b. inform the reader about the conditions under which the workmen labored.
   - ☐ c. express an opinion about the workmen.

2. From the statements below, choose those that you believe the author would agree with.
   - ☐ a. Some people will believe anything.
   - ☐ b. People in Canada and the northern region of the United States are more gullible than people elsewhere.
   - ☐ c. George Hull built the stone man to make money.

3. In this article, "What we can imagine is often more exciting and interesting than the routine of our daily lives" means
   - ☐ a. we should avoid using our imaginations so much that our day-to-day lives become boring by comparison.
   - ☐ b. the things that we can imagine are often more exciting than real life.
   - ☐ c. our daily lives are full of surprises.

4. Choose the statement below that best describes the author's position in paragraph 10.
   - ☐ a. People were justifiably angry with George Hull for creating the stone giant hoax.
   - ☐ b. Hull's hoax even fooled some experts, including those at the New York State Historical Association.
   - ☐ c. Even when people know something is a fake, they'll go to see it.

_____ Number of correct answers

Record your personal assessment of your work on the Critical Thinking Chart on page 74.

Summarizing and Paraphrasing

Put an X in the box next to the correct answer.

1. Below are summaries of the article. Choose the summary that says all the most important things about the article but in the fewest words.

☐ a. Over the years, people have been fooled by such "monsters" as the giant stone man, fur-bearing trout, and mermaids. Even after some of these hoaxes were exposed, they continued to draw crowds.

☐ b. The giant stone man, fur-bearing trout, and mermaids are fakes.

☐ c. George Hull created and buried a giant stone man. When the giant was "discovered," Hull charged people to see his fabulous fake. Other people have created and made money by exhibiting other fakes, including the fur-bearing trout, jackalope, and mermaids. These examples prove that people will flock to see fakes even after they are exposed.

2. Choose the sentence that correctly restates the following sentence from the article:

"And though the furry trout look realistic, it is surprising that people believe the farfetched stories about them."

☐ a. The trout look real, so it's not surprising that people believe the stories about them.

☐ b. Even though the trout don't look real, people believe the outrageous stories about them.

☐ c. While it's true that the furry trout look real, it's still amazing that people believe the ridiculous stories about them.

_____ Number of correct answers

Record your personal assessment of your work on the Critical Thinking Chart on page 74.

Critical Thinking

Put an X in the box next to the correct answer for questions 1 and 4. Follow the directions provided for the other questions.

1. Judging from George Hull's actions as described in this article, you can conclude that he

☐ a. felt guilty for fooling so many people.

☐ b. enjoyed the success of his elaborate hoax.

☐ c. gave the people their money back.

2. Choose from the letters below to correctly complete the following statement. Write the letters on the lines.

On the positive side, _____, but on the negative side _____.

a. the stone giant was over 10 feet tall

b. the stone giant was a fraud

c. many people enjoyed viewing what they thought was a giant from the past

3. Read paragraph 5. Then choose from the letters below to correctly complete the following statement. Write the letters on the lines.

According to paragraph 5, _____ because _____.

a. he heard a preacher speak about the giants mentioned in the Bible

b. George Hull dreamed up the idea of a stone giant

c. he made cigars from the tobacco he grew on his farm

4. What did you have to do to answer question 1?

☐ a. find a cause (why something happened)

☐ b. find a comparison (how things are the same)

☐ c. draw a conclusion (a sensible statement based on the text and your experience)

_____ Number of correct answers

Record your personal assessment of your work on the Critical Thinking Chart on page 74.

I can't really understand how

_____

_____

_____

_____

Personal Response

If I were the author, I would add

_____

_____

_____

_____

because

_____

_____

_____

_____

CRITICAL THINKING

Compare and Contrast

Think about the articles you have read in Unit One. Pick the articles that gave you the most information. Write the titles of the articles in the first column of the chart below. Use information you learned from the articles to fill in the empty boxes in the chart.

Title	When did people begin to fear this monster? Do people still fear it today?	Where was this monster said to live?	Name one idea or detail you learned from this article.

The monster that I thought was most unusual was _____ because _____

_____

_____

Words-per-Minute Table

Unit One

Directions: If you were timed while reading an article, refer to the Reading Time you recorded in the box at the end of the article. Use this words-per-minute table to determine your reading speed for that article. Then plot your reading speed on the graph on page 72.

Lesson / No. of Words	Sample 1018	1 1461	2 1450	3 973	4 1045	5 922	6 1066	7 1207	Seconds
1:30	679	974	967	648	696	615	711	805	90
1:40	611	877	870	583	626	553	640	724	100
1:50	555	797	791	530	569	503	581	658	110
2:00	509	731	725	486	522	461	533	604	120
2:10	470	674	669	449	482	426	492	557	130
2:20	436	626	621	417	447	395	457	517	140
2:30	407	584	580	389	418	369	426	483	150
2:40	382	548	544	365	392	346	400	453	160
2:50	359	516	512	343	368	325	376	426	170
3:00	339	487	483	324	348	307	355	402	180
3:10	321	461	458	307	330	291	337	381	190
3:20	305	438	435	292	313	277	320	362	200
3:30	291	417	414	278	298	263	305	345	210
3:40	278	398	395	265	285	251	291	329	220
3:50	266	381	378	254	272	241	278	315	230
4:00	255	365	363	243	261	231	267	302	240
4:10	244	351	348	233	251	221	256	290	250
4:20	235	337	335	224	241	213	246	279	260
4:30	226	325	322	216	232	205	237	268	270
4:40	218	313	311	208	224	198	228	259	280
4:50	211	302	300	201	216	191	221	250	290
5:00	204	292	290	194	209	184	213	241	300
5:10	197	283	281	188	202	178	206	234	310
5:20	191	274	272	182	196	173	200	226	320
5:30	185	266	264	177	190	168	194	219	330
5:40	180	258	256	172	184	163	188	213	340
5:50	175	250	249	167	179	158	183	207	350
6:00	170	244	242	162	174	154	178	201	360
6:10	165	237	235	158	169	150	173	196	370
6:20	161	231	229	153	165	146	168	191	380
6:30	157	225	223	150	161	142	164	186	390
6:40	153	219	218	146	157	138	160	181	400
6:50	149	214	212	142	153	135	156	177	410
7:00	145	209	207	139	149	132	152	172	420
7:10	142	204	202	136	146	129	149	168	430
7:20	139	199	198	133	142	126	145	165	440
7:30	136	195	193	130	139	123	142	161	450
7:40	133	191	189	127	136	120	139	157	460
7:50	130	187	185	124	133	118	136	154	470
8:00	127	183	181	122	131	115	133	151	480

Minutes and Seconds

Seconds

Plotting Your Progress: Reading Speed

Unit One

Directions: If you were timed while reading an article, write your words-per-minute rate for that article in the box under the number of the lesson. Then plot your reading speed on the graph by putting a small X on the line directly above the number of the lesson, across from the number of words per minute you read. As you mark your speed for each lesson, graph your progress by drawing a line to connect the X's.

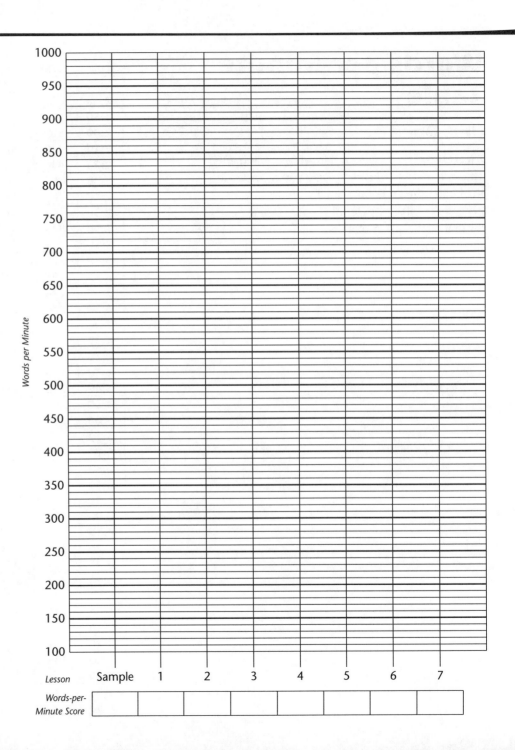

Plotting Your Progress: Reading Comprehension

Unit One

Directions: Write your Reading Comprehension score for each lesson in the box under the number of the lesson. Then plot your score on the graph by putting a small X on the line directly above the number of the lesson and across from the score you earned. As you mark your score for each lesson, graph your progress by drawing a line to connect the X's.

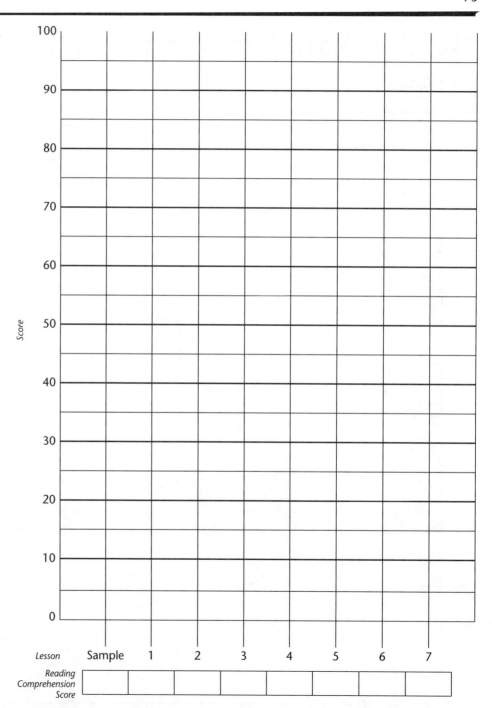

Plotting Your Progress: Critical Thinking

Unit One

Directions: Work with your teacher to evaluate your responses to the Critical Thinking questions for each lesson. Then fill in the appropriate spaces in the chart below. For each lesson and each type of Critical Thinking question, do the following: Mark a minus sign (–) in the box to indicate areas in which you feel you could improve. Mark a plus sign (+) to indicate areas in which you feel you did well. Mark a minus-slash-plus sign (–/+) to indicate areas in which you had mixed success. Then write any comments you have about your performance, including ideas for improvement.

Lesson	Author's Approach	Summarizing and Paraphrasing	Critical Thinking
Sample			
1			
2			
3			
4			
5			
6			
7			

UNIT TWO

SCYLLA AND CHARYBDIS

This painting of Scylla and Charybdis is from a fresco titled *Ulysses Cycle, painted in 1560.*

In Greek mythology, poor mortals could be crushed in an instant. They could be driven mad by a god or by some vile monster created by a god. Sailors faced many such risks. Sailing home from the Trojan War, for example, Ulysses and his men ran a gauntlet of deadly hazards. They faced Cyclops, the one-eyed monster. They had to cope with Circe, a witch-god who turned some of Ulysses' men into pigs. But two of the most fearful monsters the men faced were Scylla (SILL-uh) and Charybdis (kuh-RIB-dis).

2   Scylla was once a beautiful nymph. The sea god Glaucus fell madly in love with her. Scylla, who didn't return his affections, ran away. Desperate, the sea god asked Circe to concoct a secret love potion that would melt Scylla's heart. But Circe was herself in love with Glaucus; she didn't want him ending up in Scylla's arms. Instead, Circe tried her best to win the sea god for herself.

3   When Glaucus made it clear that he wanted nothing to do with Circe, she became furious. But she took her bitterness out on the innocent Scylla. Circe put a powerful poison in the pool in

which Scylla bathed. The next time the nymph went for a swim, the water turned the once beautiful girl into a hideous monster. Scylla grew six necks, each topped with a fierce serpent's head and armed with a triple row of fangs. Around her waist she grew six dogs' heads with razor-sharp teeth.

4   Miserable and unable to move despite the 12 legs she'd grown, Scylla soon grew to hate everything around her. Wildly sweeping her heads about, she hunted dogfish, dolphins, and whales from her rocky crag above the Strait of Messina. Scylla even reached out and snatched sailors off boats that passed too near her perch. Then she devoured them.

5   Charybdis was just as dreadful. She, too, was once a pretty young maiden— until an angry god named Zeus turned her into a monster in the form of a whirlpool. Charybdis would suck seawater in and out three times a day. Any ship caught in the grip of her swirling waters was sure to go down.

6   Scylla and Charybdis, one on each side, guarded the Strait of Messina. This waterway was so narrow that an archer could shoot an arrow from one side of the cliff bordering the strait to the other. Unfortunately, Ulysses and his crew had to pass through this strait to get back home to Greece.

7   The witch-god Circe, who apparently did have a kind side, tried to help Ulysses and his men. She not only gave them the supplies they needed but instructions on how to sail through the strait with the least possible damage. Circe told Ulysses that Scylla was "armed to the hilt with black death." But she also warned him not to go near Charybdis "when the whirlpool swallows down." If Ulysses attempted to travel through those waters, she said, then not even the gods could save him.

8   But then, Ulysses demanded, how could he pass through the strait safely? Circe said that he should "hug Scylla's crag—sail on past her—top speed! Better

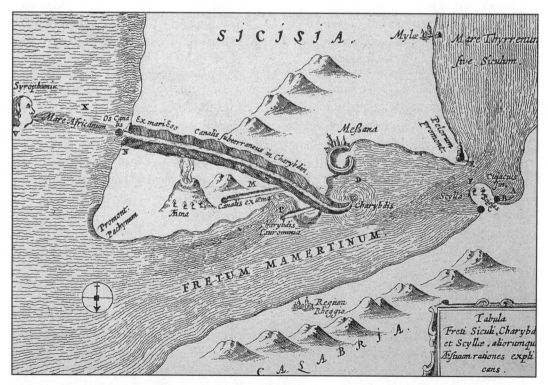

This map shows where the ancient Greeks believed the six-headed monster, Scylla, and the deadly whirlpool, Charybdis, were located.

by far to lose six men and keep your ship than lose your entire crew."

9   Ulysses, who wanted to protect his men, protested. After all, he was a mighty warrior who had defeated the Trojans and blinded the one-eyed Cyclops. "Can't I possibly cut and run from Charybdis and still fight Scylla off when she strikes my men?" he asked.

10   "You're so stubborn!" answered Circe. "Hell-bent yet again on battle and feats of arms?" Scylla, Circe reminded Ulysses, was not mortal; there was no defense against her. "Have your men row for their lives. Just flee the creature, that's the only way."

11   Ulysses told his crew as little as possible about the perils of Scylla. He didn't want his men to panic and try to hide inside the ship. Circe had told Ulysses not to arm himself. Still, old habits die hard. The warrior grabbed two spears and stood on the bow of his ship, hoping to get the first glimpse of Scylla. But the monster was nowhere to be seen.

12   With the men rowing hard, the ship entered the Strait of Messina. Scylla was on the right, Charybdis on the left. Suddenly, Charybdis sucked in the water, creating a horrible whirlpool. In the yawning abyss, the men could see nothing but rocks and sand. Ulysses and his men looked on in horror—their eyes glued on Charybdis.

13   Just then Scylla emerged from her cave within the cliff. Quickly her six heads reached out and snatched six of the toughest, strongest members of the crew. Helplessly, Ulysses turned to see his men being lifted away, their hands and feet flailing. As they rose higher and higher, they cried out in agony, "Ulysses! Ulysses!" Scylla flung each man, still writhing, onto the cliff. The evil monster then ate the men alive as they held out their hands to Ulysses in their final death struggle.

14   As Circe had predicted, the ship and the rest of the crew made it through the Strait of Messina, but their troubles were far from over. Later, the ship landed on a lush island ruled by the sun god Helios. Ulysses warned his men not to harm any of the herds belonging to Helios. At first, the crew obeyed him. But unfavorable winds kept the men stranded on the island for several weeks. Soon the supplies Circe had given them began to run low. The men grew hungry and mutinous. They wanted to kill some of the cattle and eat fresh meat. One night, while Ulysses slept, they slaughtered and ate some of the cattle.

15   When the winds changed, the ship set sail once again. Helios, however, appealed to the other gods for revenge. He got it. The gods created a great storm. Thunder and lightning destroyed the ship,

drowning all the men except Ulysses. He survived by lashing together fragments of the ship to construct a raft.

16   Unfortunately, the wind carried Ulysses back to the Strait of Messina. Charybdis sucked the frail raft into her spinning vortex. At the last possible instant, Ulysses reached up and grabbed a fig branch that grew from the side of the cliff. There, Ulysses hung as he waited for Charybdis to spit up the sea water again. When she did, Ulysses dropped down into the sea and, using just his arms, paddled away as fast as he could. Ulysses then took a moment to thank the gods for not letting Scylla see him. If she had, he said, "I'd have died on the spot." 🍃

If you have been timed while reading this article, enter your reading time below. Then turn to the Words-per-Minute Table on page 133 and look up your reading speed (words per minute). Enter your reading speed on the graph on page 134.

Reading Time: **Lesson 8**

_____ : _____

Minutes   Seconds

A | Finding the Main Idea

One statement below expresses the main idea of the article. One statement is too general, or too broad. The other statement explains only part of the article; it is too narrow. Label the statements using the following key:

M—Main Idea　　　**B—Too Broad**　　　**N—Too Narrow**

_____ 1. Scylla and Charybdis, two monsters guarding the Strait of Messina, terrorized Ulysses and his crew as they sailed home to Greece.

_____ 2. When Ulysses sailed through the Strait of Messina, Scylla devoured six of his men.

_____ 3. In Greek mythology, the gods could turn anyone they didn't like into terrible monsters.

_____ Score 15 points for a correct M answer.

_____ Score 5 points for each correct B or N answer.

_____ **Total Score:** Finding the Main Idea

B | Recalling Facts

How well do you remember the facts in the article? Put an X in the box next to the answer that correctly completes each statement about the article.

1. Scylla was turned into a monster by
   ☐ a. Glaucus.
   ☐ b. Zeus.
   ☐ c. Circe.

2. When Scylla bathed in her favorite pool, she
   ☐ a. grew six necks with a serpent's head on each one.
   ☐ b. changed into a whirlpool.
   ☐ c. was turned into a pig.

3. In order to pass through the Strait of Messina safely, Circe told Ulysses to
   ☐ a. arm himself against Scylla.
   ☐ b. sail close to Charybdis.
   ☐ c. sail close to Scylla.

4. As Ulysses' ship sailed through the strait,
   ☐ a. Charybdis sucked six of the crew into the sea.
   ☐ b. Scylla grabbed and devoured six of the crew.
   ☐ c. thunder and lightning destroyed the ship.

5. As he floated through the Strait of Messina on a raft, Ulysses was saved from being sucked into the whirlpool by
   ☐ a. Helios.
   ☐ b. Scylla.
   ☐ c. a fig branch growing on the side of the cliff.

Score 5 points for each correct answer.

_____ **Total Score:** Recalling Facts

C | Making Inferences

When you combine your own experience and information from a text to draw a conclusion that is not directly stated in that text, you are making an inference. Below are five statements that may or may not be inferences based on information in the article. Label the statements using the following key:

C—Correct Inference   **F—Faulty Inference**

_____ 1. Ulysses cared deeply about the men on his ship.

_____ 2. The gods in Greek myths were always kind and fair.

_____ 3. Ulysses didn't know that his men had killed and eaten some of the sun god's cattle.

_____ 4. Scylla and Charybdis were evil even before they were turned into monsters.

_____ 5. Circe liked Ulysses.

Score 5 points for each correct answer.

_____ **Total Score:** Making Inferences

D | Using Words Precisely

Each numbered sentence below contains an underlined word or phrase from the article. Following the sentence are three definitions. One definition is closest to the meaning of the underlined word. One definition is opposite or nearly opposite. Label those two definitions using the following key. Do not label the remaining definition.

C—Closest   **O—Opposite or Nearly Opposite**

1. They could be driven mad by a god or by some <u>vile</u> monster created by a god.

    _____ a. young

    _____ b. noble

    _____ c. evil

2. Desperate, the sea god asked Circe to <u>concoct</u> a secret love potion that would melt Scylla's heart.

    _____ a. drink

    _____ b. prepare

    _____ c. destroy

3. Ulysses told his crew as little as possible about the <u>perils</u> of Scylla.

    _____ a. danger

    _____ b. legend

    _____ c. security

4. In the yawning <u>abyss</u>, the men could see nothing but rocks and sand.

    _____ a. widest sea

    _____ b. extremely deep pit

    _____ c. tallest mountain

5. The men grew hungry and <u>mutinous</u>.

_____ a. obedient

_____ b. rebellious

_____ c. exhausted

_____ Score 3 points for each correct C answer.

_____ Score 2 points for each correct O answer.

_____ **Total Score:** Using Words Precisely

Enter the four total scores in the spaces below, and add them together to find your Reading Comprehension Score. Then record your score on the graph on page 135.

Score	Question Type	Lesson 8
_____	Finding the Main Idea	
_____	Recalling Facts	
_____	Making Inferences	
_____	Using Words Precisely	
_____	**Reading Comprehension Score**	

Author's Approach

Put an X in the box next to the correct answer.

1. The main purpose of the first paragraph is to

☐ a. inform the reader about Scylla and Charybdis only.

☐ b. describe the role Ulysses played in the Trojan War.

☐ c. make the reader aware of some of the monsters in Greek mythology.

2. Which of the following statements from the article best describes Ulysses?

☐ a. "After all, he was a mighty warrior who had defeated the Trojans and blinded the one-eyed Cyclops."

☐ b. "Helplessly, Ulysses turned to see his men being lifted away, their hands and feet flailing."

☐ c. "Ulysses and his men looked on in horror—their eyes glued on Charybdis."

3. From the statements below, choose those that you believe the author would agree with.

☐ a. Ulysses was brave and resourceful.

☐ b. The gods sometimes acted cruel and heartless.

☐ c. The gods would never harm Ulysses, no matter what he did.

4. In this article, "Sailing home from the Trojan War, for example, Ulysses and his men ran a gauntlet of deadly hazards" means

☐ a. many of Ulysses' crew died on the trip home.

☐ b. Ulysses and his crew encountered many life-threatening situations on their trip home.

☐ c. Ulysses and his crew fought many deadly battles in the Trojan War.

_____ Number of correct answers

Record your personal assessment of your work on the Critical Thinking Chart on page 136.

CRITICAL THINKING

Summarizing and Paraphrasing

Put an X in the box next to the correct answer.

1. Below are summaries of the article. Choose the summary that says all the most important things about the article but in the fewest words.

☐ a. Circe helped Ulysses and his men sail their ship through the Strait of Messina, which was guarded by two terrible monsters called Scylla and Charybdis. Later, when Ulysses attempted to pass through the waterway alone on a raft, he narrowly escaped from both monsters again.

☐ b. Scylla and Charybdis were turned into monsters by Greek gods. Ulysses faced the monsters when he and his men sailed through the Strait of Messina on their way home to Greece. Although Ulysses and most of his men passed safely through the waterway, six of his crew were eaten by Scylla.

☐ c. Although Ulysses escaped from the two monsters guarding the Strait of Messina, six of his men were snatched from the ship and devoured by Scylla.

2. Choose the sentence that correctly restates the following sentence from the article:

"But Circe was herself in love with Glaucus; she didn't want him ending up in Scylla's arms."

☐ a. Scylla was in love with Glaucus and didn't want him to be with Circe.

☐ b. Glaucus was in love with Circe and didn't want him to be with Scylla.

☐ c. Circe was in love with Glaucus and didn't want him to be with Scylla.

_____ Number of correct answers

Record your personal assessment of your work on the Critical Thinking Chart on page 136.

Critical Thinking

Follow the directions provided for questions 1, 2, and 4. Put an X in the box next to the correct answer for question 3.

1. Using what is told about Scylla and Charybdis in the article, name three ways Scylla is similar to Charybdis and three ways Scylla is different from Charybdis. Cite the paragraph number(s) where you found details in the article to support your conclusions.

Similarities

_____

_____

_____

Differences

_____

_____

_____

2. Think about cause-effect relationships in the article. Fill in the blanks in the cause-effect chart, drawing from the letters below.

Cause	Effect
_____	The witch-god poisoned Scylla's pool.
_____	The men ate some of Helios's herd.
Ulysses held onto a fig branch.	_____

a. Ulysses and his men were stranded on an island, and their supplies ran low.

b. Glaucus fell in love with Scylla and rejected Circe.

c. The mighty warrior survived Charybdis and her spinning vortex.

3. How are Scylla and Charybdis examples of monsters?

☐ a. They are evil, deformed creatures who show their victims no mercy.

☐ b. They were turned into monsters by Greek gods.

☐ c. They were once beautiful young maidens.

4. Which paragraphs from the article provide evidence that supports your answer to question 2?

_____

_____

_____ Number of correct answers

Record your personal assessment of your work on the Critical Thinking Chart on page 136.

Self-Assessment

Before reading this article, I already knew

_____

_____

_____

_____

Personal Response

How do you think Ulysses felt when his men were devoured by Scylla?

_____

_____

_____

FRANKENSTEIN'S MONSTER

The young scientist stood alone in his workroom. The only sound in the room was that of rain beating rhythmically against the windowpanes. Suddenly the scientist jumped back in horror. The body that had been lying lifeless on the table was beginning to move. The creature slowly lifted its lids to reveal dull yellow eyes. Its limbs began to twitch, and it started to breathe.

2   Terrified, the scientist stared at the strange man that he had created. The creature was eight feet tall and had long arms and large hands. His skin was patched and sewn together in many places, and his lips were black. The scientist had hoped that his man would be beautiful. But as he watched him come to life, he saw that his creation was a miserable and disgusting creature.

3   This is probably the most famous scene in the story of Frankenstein. When that story is mentioned, most people immediately recall the movie versions. But Dr. Frankenstein's' dreadful monster was born not in a movie, but in a book. The novel, entitled *Frankenstein*, was written in 1816. In that book, the monster has no name. The young scientist who created him is named Victor Frankenstein. Over the years, people have mistakenly come to refer to the monster as Frankenstein.

4   The author of *Frankenstein* was 18-year-old Mary Wollstonecraft Shelley. Mary Shelley began *Frankenstein* one summer while she and her future husband, the poet Percy Shelley, were vacationing in Switzerland. They were visiting the famous poet Lord Byron. On rainy days, the friends would entertain themselves by reading ghost stories aloud. One night, when they'd again been trapped indoors by a storm, the group was reading a particularly boring German ghost story. To liven things up, Byron proposed a contest. He challenged each of his companions to write a better ghost story than the one they were currently reading. Mary Shelley's story was, of course, *Frankenstein*. It took her 11 months to write.

5   The full title of Shelley's novel is *Frankenstein, or The Modern Prometheus*. The original Prometheus was a lesser Greek god who gave humans the gift of fire. Zeus, the king of the gods, felt that Prometheus's gift made humans too powerful. Prometheus had taken too much power unto himself. For that, Zeus decided to punish the weaker god. He chained Prometheus to the side of a mountain to be tortured by eagles. When Shelley calls Frankenstein a modern Prometheus, she is suggesting that, like Prometheus, the scientist had gone too far. He had done what only God had the right to do—create life. Also like Prometheus, Victor Frankenstein suffers terribly for daring to play God.

Frankenstein is a popular subject for Hollywood movies. On the far left is Boris Karloff as the monster from the 1931 movie Frankenstein. *On the left is Elsa Lanchester in the 1935 film* The Bride of Frankenstein.

Mary Shelley created the Frankenstein story in 1816, while vacationing in Switzerland.

6   The story of Frankenstein and his monster begins in Switzerland. It was there that the scientist received his education and began to devote himself to the mystery of the creation of life. He conducted many experiments, using bodies that he stole from cemeteries. Frankenstein finally learned the secret of life, and found that he was able to bring the spark of life to non-living material.

7   So the scientist went to work to create a new man. Shutting himself off from his family and friends, he spent endless hours in his laboratory. He emerged only to raid cemeteries for organs and limbs. He worked day and night, wrecking his health. At last he succeeded in bringing the creature to life. But as soon as he had done so, he was filled with regret. He fled in horror from the monster. Then he suffered a nervous breakdown.

8   What Frankenstein did not take the time to discover was that the monster was a kind and gentle soul. He wanted to be loved and to take part in the world of men. But his hideous form made everyone, even his creator, run from him in fear. In pain and anger then, the creature turned to violence.

9   After a time, Frankenstein regained his health. But tragedy soon struck. His younger brother was strangled by an unknown murderer. Quickly Victor traveled to the scene of his brother's death. As he stood there in the dark, a flash of lightning cut across the sky. In that eerie light, Victor saw a grotesque figure outlined against the sky. It was his monster. In that brief, terrible moment, Frankenstein knew that it was his creation that had killed his brother.

10   Victor told no one of his discovery. He did not dare reveal that he had created a monster. Even when an innocent man was hanged as his brother's killer, he maintained his silence. During that period, Victor thought often of ending his own life. But he realized that he was the only one who could save his friends and family from future attacks by the monster.

11   Then the creature went to Frankenstein. He had learned to speak, and he used his new ability to make a terrible demand. He ordered Victor to create a female companion for him. He warned that if Frankenstein refused, he would begin killing the other members of his family. In the face of that threat, Frankenstein agreed to make a mate for the monster. In return, the creature promised never again to have anything to do with humans.

12   Dr. Frankenstein created the female monster, as he had promised. But as he finished his work, he was overcome with serious misgivings. What if this male–female pair mated to breed a race of hideous creatures? To prevent such a tragedy, Frankenstein destroyed the female. When the monster discovered the death of his mate, he swore a terrible revenge, and then vanished.

13   The monster's revenge was swift. He murdered both Victor's bride and his best friend. In response, Frankenstein pursued the monster all over the world, seeking to destroy it. The monster led him across the treacherous ice of the Arctic Ocean. The creature finally got away when the ice broke apart and separated him from Frankenstein. Victor was rescued by a whaling ship, but he died soon after.

14   Borne on a chunk of floating ice, the monster drifted to the ship that carried his creator's body. There he wept for what he had done and for what had been done to him—for the hopeless life that he had been given. He vowed that he would punish himself. In so doing, he would also free himself from misery. He said that he would build a funeral pyre and destroy himself by setting himself afire. Then he got back on the chunk of ice and floated away, never to be seen again.

If you have been timed while reading this article, enter your reading time below. Then turn to the Words-per-Minute Table on page 133 and look up your reading speed (words per minute). Enter your reading speed on the graph on page 134.

Reading Time: **Lesson 9**

_____ : _____

Minutes   *Seconds*

A | Finding the Main Idea

One statement below expresses the main idea of the article. One statement is too general, or too broad. The other statement explains only part of the article; it is too narrow. Label the statements using the following key:

M—Main Idea   **B—Too Broad**   **N—Too Narrow**

_____ 1. *Frankenstein* is a chilling monster story that remains popular more than 150 years after it was created.

_____ 2. Mary Wollstonecraft Shelley wrote the story of Frankenstein in 1816, when she was just 18 years old, as an entry in a friendly contest.

_____ 3. *Frankenstein* originated as a novel in which a horrible and pathetic monster is created by a scientist who wants the power to create life.

_____ Score 15 points for a correct M answer.

_____ Score 5 points for each correct B or N answer.

_____ **Total Score:** Finding the Main Idea

B | Recalling Facts

How well do you remember the facts in the article? Put an X in the box next to the answer that correctly completes each statement about the article.

1. In the original title for her novel, Mary Shelley compared Victor Frankenstein to
   ☐ a. a monster.
   ☐ b. Zeus.
   ☐ c. Prometheus.

2. Frankenstein destroyed the female he created because
   ☐ a. he wanted to punish his monster.
   ☐ b. he was afraid that she would breed more monsters.
   ☐ c. she was a hideous creature.

3. Victor Frankenstein died
   ☐ a. on an ice floe in the Arctic.
   ☐ b. in his monster's arms.
   ☐ c. after he boarded a whaling ship.

4. When he first came to life, Frankenstein's monster was
   ☐ a. ugly but kind and gentle.
   ☐ b. ugly and violent.
   ☐ c. sad and ugly.

5. The first person that the monster killed was Frankenstein's
   ☐ a. friend.
   ☐ b. brother.
   ☐ c. bride.

Score 5 points for each correct answer.

_____ **Total Score:** Recalling Facts

C | Making Inferences

When you combine your own experience and information from a text to draw a conclusion that is not directly stated in that text, you are making an inference. Below are five statements that may or may not be inferences based on information in the article. Label the statements using the following key:

C—Correct Inference   **F—Faulty Inference**

_____ 1. Mary Shelley was the most gifted writer of the friends who vacationed together.

_____ 2. More movies have been made about Frankenstein's monster than about any other monster.

_____ 3. If Victor Frankenstein had not been horrified by the ugliness of his creation, the monster might not have become violent.

_____ 4. The story of Frankenstein is a modern retelling of a Greek myth.

_____ 5. Mary Shelley was familiar with Greek mythology.

Score 5 points for each correct answer.

_____ **Total Score:** Making Inferences

D | Using Words Precisely

Each numbered sentence below contains an underlined word or phrase from the article. Following the sentence are three definitions. One definition is closest to the meaning of the underlined word. One definition is opposite or nearly opposite. Label those two definitions using the following key. Do not label the remaining definition.

C—Closest   **O—Opposite or Nearly Opposite**

1. In that eerie light, Victor saw a grotesque figure outlined against the sky.

_____ a. finely built

_____ b. barely visible

_____ c. monstrous

2. But as he finished his work, he was overcome with serious misgivings.

_____ a. doubts

_____ b. illnesses

_____ c. certainties

3. He emerged only to raid cemeteries for organs and limbs.

_____ a. spoke

_____ b. came out

_____ c. stayed inside

4. Even when an innocent man was hanged as his brother's killer, he maintained his silence.

_____ a. gave up

_____ b. kept up

_____ c. proved

5. <u>Borne on</u> his own chunk of floating ice, the monster drifted to the ship that carried his creator's body.

_____ a. thrown off

_____ b. defeated by

_____ c. carried along on

_____ Score 3 points for each correct C answer.

_____ Score 2 points for each correct O answer.

_____ **Total Score:** Using Words Precisely

Enter the four total scores in the spaces below, and add them together to find your Reading Comprehension Score. Then record your score on the graph on page 135.

Score	Question Type	Lesson 9
_____	Finding the Main Idea	
_____	Recalling Facts	
_____	Making Inferences	
_____	Using Words Precisely	
_____	**Reading Comprehension Score**	

Author's Approach

Put an X in the box next to the correct answer.

1. What does the author mean by the statement "Also like Prometheus, Victor Frankenstein suffered terribly for daring to play God"?

☐ a. Frankenstein challenged God to play a game with him, and the scientist lost badly.

☐ b. Frankenstein paid a harsh penalty for daring to create life.

☐ c. Like Prometheus, Frankenstein was also tortured by eagles.

2. Which of the following statements from the article best describes the personality of Frankenstein's monster?

☐ a. "The creature was eight feet tall and had long arms and large hands."

☐ b. "His skin was patched and sewn together in many places, and his lips were black."

☐ c. "He wanted to be loved and to take part in the world of men."

3. Choose the statement below that best describes the author's position in paragraph 8.

☐ a. The monster would have been a good creature if Frankenstein had loved him.

☐ b. The monster would have killed Frankenstein if the scientist had not run away.

☐ c. The monster would have turned into a cruel killer no matter what Frankenstein did.

4. The author probably wrote this article in order to

☐ a. retell the story of Frankenstein and his creation.

☐ b. inform the reader about Mary Shelley's life.

☐ c. compare the monster's portrayal in the book to that in movies.

_____ Number of correct answers

Record your personal assessment of your work on the Critical Thinking Chart on page 136.

Summarizing and Paraphrasing

Follow the directions provided for questions 1 and 2. Put an X in the box next to the correct answer for question 3.

1. Look for the important ideas and events in paragraphs 11 and 12. Summarize those paragraphs in one or two sentences.

_____

_____

_____

2. Complete the following one-sentence summary of the article using the lettered phrases from the phrase bank below. Write the letters on the lines.

> **Phrase Bank:**
> a. a description of the circumstances surrounding Mary Shelley's creation of the story
> b. the story's main conflict—the clash between Victor Frankenstein and his monster
> c. Victor's death and the monster's disappearance

After a short introduction, the article about Frankenstein's monster begins with _____, goes on to explain _____, and ends with _____.

3. Read the statement about the article below. Then read the paraphrase of that statement. Choose the reason that best tells why the paraphrase does not say the same thing as the statement.

Statement: Mary Shelley's novel compares Victor Frankenstein to the Greek god Prometheus; both suffered because they tried to become too powerful.

Paraphrase: Mary Shelley's book draws a comparison between her main character and Prometheus.

☐ a. Paraphrase says too much.

☐ b. Paraphrase doesn't say enough.

☐ c. Paraphrase doesn't agree with the statement about the article.

_____ Number of correct answers

Record your personal assessment of your work on the Critical Thinking Chart on page 136.

Critical Thinking

Put an X in the box next to the correct answer for questions 1, 3, and 4. Follow the directions provided for the other question.

1. From what the monster said, you can predict that if Frankenstein had not destroyed the monster's bride, the monster would

☐ a. have killed Victor's bride and best friend anyway.

☐ b. not have killed Victor's bride and best friend.

☐ c. have killed his new companion.

2. Choose from the letters below to correctly complete the following statement. Write the letters on the lines.

In the article, _____ and _____ are alike.

a. the monster

b. Prometheus

c. Victor Frankenstein

3. What was the effect of Byron's suggesting that the friends have a ghost story contest?

☐ a. Mary Shelley wrote *Frankenstein*.

☐ b. The group read a particularly boring German ghost story.

☐ c. Mary and Percy Shelley vacationed in Switzerland.

4. How is Victor Frankenstein's creation an example of a monster?

☐ a. Many horror movies featuring the creature have been made.

☐ b. The creature was made in a laboratory.

☐ c. The creature was hideous and violent.

_____ Number of correct answers

Record your personal assessment of your work on the Critical Thinking Chart on page 136.

Personal Response

I wonder why

_____

_____

_____

Self-Assessment

The part I found most difficult about the article was

_____

_____

_____

I found this difficult because

_____

_____

_____

_____

CRITICA

THE MINOTAUR
Beast of the Labyrinth

This is the Bull Portico of the Palace of Knossos on the Greek island of Crete. The famous labyrinth from Greek mythology in which Theseus encountered the Minotaur was based on the floor plan of this palace.

Theseus was the son of Aegeus, king of Athens. But he was born and raised in his mother's home in a city in southern Greece, far from Athens. As a child, he never met his father, for the king returned to Athens before the boy was born. Just before leaving, Aegeus placed a sword and sandals under a large stone and instructed his wife to send their son to Athens when the boy was strong enough to move the stone and remove the objects beneath it. "I will recognize the sword and sandals," Aegeus told his wife, "and I will know that the one who bears them is my son and that he has grown into a tall, strong man."

2   Over the years, Theseus's mother watched her son grow, until finally she thought the time was right. Then she took him to the stone, and he cast it away with ease. Taking the sword and sandals, the young man set out for his father's kingdom.

3   When Theseus reached Athens, he was met by Aegeus, who was delighted to see his son at last. The time for joy was short,

however, for Theseus had arrived in Athens at the worst possible time. King Minos of the island of Crete was looking for 14 new victims for the Minotaur.

4 On Crete, King Minos kept a terrible beast, half man and half bull, called the Minotaur. It lived within an enormous maze called the Labyrinth. The Labyrinth was cleverly constructed, with miles and miles of winding passages, unexpected turnings, and dead ends. It was so complex, in fact, that people who were put into it could never find their way out. They simply wandered until the Minotaur found and devoured them. To satisfy the Minotaur's appetite, Minos put seven young men and seven maidens into the maze each year.

5 The victims were always collected from Athens. Years before, King Minos had sent his only son on a visit to Athens. While the young man was there, King Aegeus sent him on a mission to kill a dangerous bull. He was killed by the bull. In a rage, Minos invaded Athens and declared that he would destroy it unless every year the people sent him seven men and seven maidens to sacrifice to the Minotaur.

6 When Theseus learned of the situation, he offered himself as one of the victims. Aegeus begged him not to go, but the young man would not listen to his father's entreaties. Theseus told him that

he was confident that he could defeat the Minotaur. So when the victims' ship set sail for Crete, Theseus was on board.

7 They set out with the wind filling the black sail that was customarily used for the ship carrying victims to the Minotaur. Theseus promised his father that when he returned he would replace the black sail with a white one, so that Aegeus would know long before his son set foot in Athens again that he was safe.

8 When the Athenian ship reached Crete, the 14 victims were presented to King Minos and his daughter, Ariadne. As soon as Ariadne looked upon the handsome Theseus, she fell deeply in love with him. Ariadne went secretly to Daedalus, who had constructed the Labyrinth, and asked him to show her a way to get out of it. Then she sent for Theseus and told him she would help him escape if he would promise to marry her and take her back to Athens with him. Theseus readily agreed.

9 In accordance with the clue she had been given, Ariadne secretly gave Theseus a ball of string. She told him to tie it to the gate when he entered the Labyrinth, and to unroll it as he went along. He need only follow it back to find his way out. Then Ariadne told him one other thing. The Minotaur could be slain only if its brain was pierced by one of its own horns.

10 As Theseus entered the Labyrinth with the other victims, he unwound the ball of string as he had been instructed. He traveled the twisting, turning passageways of the maze until he sensed that he was nearing the center. Then, from up ahead, he heard a stamping of hooves that made the earth tremble. The Minotaur was near.

Theseus and the Minotaur

11   Theseus advanced slowly around the next few corners. At last the walls of the Labyrinth opened into a wide courtyard with a circular hedge of prickly briars in the center. Theseus listened for some clue to the monster's position, but there was only silence. Theseus sensed that from somewhere behind the briars two evil eyes were watching him.

12   Suddenly, with a mighty roar, the Minotaur burst from behind the hedge. It charged toward Theseus with its head down and its two great horns flashing in the sunlight. As the beast rushed forward, it appeared that Theseus would surely be impaled on its deadly horns. But the youth was ready for the attack. When the Minotaur was just a few feet from him, Theseus stepped aside, and as the beast flashed by, Theseus grabbed one of its horns in a wrestler's grip. He twisted his body sharply, throwing all his weight to one side. With a crack like a branch being torn from an oak tree in a windstorm, the horn was wrenched from its socket. The Minotaur bellowed in pain and rage.

13   Before the monster could collect itself to charge again, Theseus lifted the horn high and thrust it with all his might at the Minotaur's head. The horn shot through the monster's skull and pierced its brain. The Minotaur uttered a terrible cry that was part animal and part human. Then it dropped to the ground, felled by the very weapon that it had used to take so many lives.

14   Remembering Ariadne's instructions, Theseus then quickly began following the cord back along the passageways through which he had traveled. He easily made his way out of the Labyrinth. Ariadne and the thirteen Athenians were overjoyed at Theseus's success. Together they made their way back to the ship and sailed for Athens.

15   On the homeward journey, they stopped at the island of Naxos. While the young people were resting, the goddess Athena appeared to Theseus in a dream. She said that Ariadne was destined to wed a god and that Theseus must not come between the princess and her fate. So Theseus left Ariadne on Naxos and set sail again for Athens.

16   As the ship neared the coast of Athens, Theseus forgot about the signal he had arranged with his father. He neglected to pull down the black sail and raise the white one. King Aegeus, anxious about his son, had been standing for days on a cliff above the sea, scanning the horizon for the returning ship. When he caught sight of the vessel coming toward him under a black sail, the king was overcome with grief. In his anguish, he threw himself into the sea and was killed. From that day on, the sea was called the Aegean.

17   When Theseus arrived in Athens, he mourned the death of his father. The people praised him as a hero for killing the Minotaur, and he was made king. 🍃

If you have been timed while reading this article, enter your reading time below. Then turn to the Words-per-Minute Table on page 133 and look up your reading speed (words per minute). Enter your reading speed on the graph on page 134.

Reading Time: Lesson 10

_____ : _____

Minutes   Seconds

A Finding the Main Idea

One statement below expresses the main idea of the article. One statement is too general, or too broad. The other statement explains only part of the article; it is too narrow. Label the statements using the following key:

M—Main Idea   **B—Too Broad**   **N—Too Narrow**

_____ 1. Theseus marked his path through the Labyrinth by unwinding a ball of string as he walked.

_____ 2. Against great odds, Theseus destroyed a terrible monster.

_____ 3. By destroying the terrible Minotaur, a monster who devoured humans, a young man named Theseus became a hero in Athens.

_____ Score 15 points for a correct M answer.

_____ Score 5 points for each correct B or N answer.

_____ **Total Score:** Finding the Main Idea

B Recalling Facts

How well do you remember the facts in the article? Put an X in the box next to the answer that correctly completes each statement about the article.

1. When the ship set sail for the island of Crete, it was under a
   - ☐ a. black sail.
   - ☐ b. red sail.
   - ☐ c. white sail.

2. Ariadne had obtained the secret to getting out of the Labyrinth from
   - ☐ a. Daedalus.
   - ☐ b. King Aegeus.
   - ☐ c. Athena.

3. Theseus found the Minotaur
   - ☐ a. hiding behind a hedge of briars.
   - ☐ b. peering out of a cave.
   - ☐ c. in a narrow passage of the Labyrinth.

4. Theseus used the Minotaur's horn to
   - ☐ a. cut off its head.
   - ☐ b. stab its heart.
   - ☐ c. puncture its brain.

5. Athena told Theseus to give up Ariadne so that the girl could
   - ☐ a. return to her father.
   - ☐ b. become her servant.
   - ☐ c. marry a god.

Score 5 points for each correct answer.

_____ **Total Score:** Recalling Facts

C | Making Inferences

When you combine your own experience and information from a text to draw a conclusion that is not directly stated in that text, you are making an inference. Below are five statements that may or may not be inferences based on information in the article. Label the statements using the following key:

C—Correct Inference   **F—Faulty Inference**

_____ 1. The Labyrinth covered most of the island of Crete.

_____ 2. Theseus was a fearless young man.

_____ 3. Theseus agreed to take Ariadne back to Athens with him because he loved her.

_____ 4. Theseus left the black sail up on purpose, because he knew that his father would kill himself and he would become king.

_____ 5. Ariadne did not know that it was her destiny to marry a god.

Score 5 points for each correct answer.

_____ **Total Score:** Making Inferences

D | Using Words Precisely

Each numbered sentence below contains an underlined word or phrase from the article. Following the sentence are three definitions. One definition is closest to the meaning of the underlined word. One definition is opposite or nearly opposite. Label those two definitions using the following key. Do not label the remaining definition.

C—Closest   **O—Opposite or Nearly Opposite**

1. Aegeus begged him not to go, but the young man would not listen to his father's <u>entreaties</u>.

   _____ a. pleadings

   _____ b. orders

   _____ c. dreams

2. <u>In accordance</u> with the clue she had been given, Ariadne secretly gave Theseus a ball of string.

   _____ a. in opposition

   _____ b. in agreement

   _____ c. in all

3. Then it dropped to the ground, <u>felled</u> by the very weapon that it had used to take so many lives.

   _____ a. brought down

   _____ b. propped up

   _____ c. tripped over

4. She said that Ariadne was <u>destined</u> to wed a god, and that Theseus must not come between the princess and her fate.

_____ a. not meant

_____ b. anxious

_____ c. fated

5. In his <u>anguish</u>, he threw himself into the sea and was killed.

_____ a. great sorrow

_____ b. rage

_____ c. joy

_____ Score 3 points for each correct C answer.

_____ Score 2 points for each correct O answer.

_____ **Total Score:** Using Words Precisely

Enter the four total scores in the spaces below, and add them together to find your Reading Comprehension Score. Then record your score on the graph on page 135.

Score	Question Type	Lesson 10
_____	Finding the Main Idea	
_____	Recalling Facts	
_____	Making Inferences	
_____	Using Words Precisely	
_____	**Reading Comprehension Score**	

Author's Approach

Put an X in the box next to the correct answer.

1. The main purpose of the first paragraph is to

☐ a. describe the geography of ancient Greece.

☐ b. explain why Theseus would travel to Athens as a young man.

☐ c. describe Theseus's strength.

2. What is the author's purpose in writing "The Minotaur: Beast of the Labyrinth"?

☐ a. To inform the reader about Theseus's encounter with the Minotaur

☐ b. To describe terrible monsters of Greek mythology

☐ c. To compare King Aegeus to King Minos

3. From the statements below, choose those that you believe the author would agree with.

☐ a. King Minos was a vengeful, cruel ruler.

☐ b. Theseus would have been able to kill the Minotaur without Ariadne's help.

☐ c. Theseus did not want to anger the gods.

4. What does the author imply by saying "When he caught sight of the vessel coming toward him under a black sail, the king was overcome with grief"?

☐ a. The king thought that the Minotaur was dead.

☐ b. The king thought that Ariadne was dead.

☐ c. The king thought that his son was dead.

_____ Number of correct answers

Record your personal assessment of your work on the Critical Thinking Chart on page 136.

CRITICAL THINKING

Summarizing and Paraphrasing

Follow the directions provided for question 1. Put an X in the box next to the correct answer for question 2.

1. Reread paragraph 4 in the article. Below, write a summary of the paragraph in no more than 25 words.

_____

_____

_____

Reread your summary and decide whether it covers the important ideas in the paragraph. Next, decide how to shorten the summary to 15 words or less without leaving out any essential information. Write this summary below.

_____

_____

_____

2. Choose the best one-sentence paraphrase for the following sentence from the article:

    "In a rage, Minos invaded Athens and declared that he would destroy it unless every year the people sent him seven men and seven maidens to sacrifice to the Minotaur."

☐ a. Minos claimed that he would destroy the Minotaur if the people of Athens didn't send him 14 human sacrifices every year.

☐ b. An angry Minos declared that he would destroy seven men and seven maidens every year if Athens did not destroy the Minotaur.

☐ c. Minos claimed that he would destroy Athens if the people of the city did not send him 14 human sacrifices every year.

_____   Number of correct answers

Record your personal assessment of your work on the Critical Thinking Chart on page 136.

Critical Thinking

Put an X in the box next to the correct answer for questions 1 and 4. Follow the directions provided for the other questions.

1. From what the article told about Ariadne, you can conclude that she was

☐ a. heartbroken when Theseus left her behind in Naxos.

☐ b. excited about the prospect of marrying a god.

☐ c. glad to be rid of Theseus.

2. Choose from the letters below to correctly complete the following statement. Write the letters on the lines.

On the positive side, _____, but on the negative side _____.

   a.   Theseus forgot to change the flag and caused his father's death

   b.   Ariadne fell in love with Theseus

   c.   Theseus was successful in killing the Minotaur

3. Think about cause-effect relationships in the article. Fill in the blanks in the cause-effect chart, drawing from the letters below.

Cause	Effect
Minos's son was killed by a bull.	_____
_____	Theseus was able to kill the Minotaur.
_____	Aegeus threw himself into the sea.

   a.   Ariadne told him how to defeat the monster.

   b.   The king forced Athenians to make annual sacrifices to the Minotaur.

   c.   Theseus forgot to pull down the black sail and raise the white one.

4. How is the Minotaur an example of a monster?

☐ a.   The Minotaur lived in an enormous maze.

☐ b.   The Minotaur was half man and half bull.

☐ c.   The Minotaur could only be killed by one of its own horns.

5. Which paragraphs from the article provide evidence that supports your answer to question 3?

_____ Number of correct answers

Record your personal assessment of your work on the Critical Thinking Chart on page 136.

Personal Response

How do you think you would feel if you had to face the Minotaur?

_____

_____

_____

_____

Self-Assessment

One of the things I did best when reading this article was

_____

_____

_____

_____

I believe I did this well because

_____

_____

_____

_____

CRITICAL THINKING

GIANTS
Fact or Myth?

The story of David and Goliath has been the subject of many pieces of fine art throughout the centuries. Michelangelo Caravaggio painted David with the Head of Goliath in 1607.

Thousands of years ago, people from all parts of the world believed in the existence of giants. Over time, stories of the giants were passed down to new generations. Many of those stories are still with us today. Most people think the tales are ridiculous, of course. But there are those who believe that the stories are true. They believe that in early days a race of giants did roam the earth. Many kinds of evidence are offered to support the idea that giants truly existed.

2   One source of evidence is the Bible. The Bible contains several stories of giants. Probably the most famous is the one about the Philistine giant, Goliath. According to the Bible, Goliath stood "six cubits and a span," or 10 feet nine inches tall. He wore a coat of armor and carried a sword and shield. When a young Hebrew shepherd named David set out to fight the fierce giant, it seemed certain that Goliath would win. David was much smaller than Goliath, and was armed only with a sling—a short leather strap with a string attached to each end, used for throwing stones. With his sling, David could hurl a

stone with great speed and accuracy. Even so, he seemed no match for the mighty Goliath.

3   When Goliath and David confronted each other, the young shepherd picked up a small, smooth stone. Aiming at the one unprotected part of the giant's body—his forehead—David placed the stone in his sling and whirled the simple weapon over his head. He let the stone fly, and it struck Goliath directly on the forehead. As a result of that blow, the Bible says, the giant "fell to his face upon the earth."

4   Another legendary giant from Biblical times was Og, king of Bashan. Og is said to have lived for three thousand years. He supposedly survived the Great Flood of Noah's time by climbing on the roof of the ark. In the daytime, Og waded along beside the ark. At night Noah let him use the ark's roof as a bed. Og scooped fish out of the floodwaters for food. He roasted the fish by holding them up to the sun.

5   According to a Hebrew myth, Og finally died when he quarreled with the ancient Hebrews. In his anger, he picked up a mountain to throw at his enemies. He became so entangled in his burden, however, that Moses was able to kill him. Legend says that the ancient Hebrews then took one of Og's bones and used it to bridge a river.

6   Giants appear in the myths of almost all cultures. The ancient Greeks believed in a race of giants called the Cyclopes (seye-CLO-peez). A Cyclops was thought to be a huge, primitive creature with one eye in the middle of its forehead. Most ancient Greeks were quick to admit that they had never actually seen a living cyclops. But many believed that they had seen the skull of one of the monsters. The skull, which was kept in a special place, was enormous. It had what appeared to be a single eye socket centered in its forehead.

7   Today most scientists are convinced that the skull did not belong to a cyclops. What the Greeks thought was the skull of a giant one-eyed monster was really the skull of an elephant. The confusion began when someone took an elephant skull from Africa to Greece. There were no elephants in Greece, and the Greeks had no way of knowing about the huge beasts. The elephant skull had a big opening in the center, where the trunk had joined the head. It was logical for the Greeks to assume that the opening in the skull was the socket of a one-eyed giant.

8   Today people who believe in giants often point to the great pyramids of Egypt as proof that enormous people once lived on earth. The pyramids, and the stone Sphinx that guards them, were built over four thousand years ago. Since heavy construction machinery did not exist in those days, it is hard to imagine

This mural from the King Arthur Cycle in the summer-house of Runkelstein Castle depicts three giants between a group of knights in armor, while a third knight greets King Arthur.

how those mammoth structures were erected. Some people argue that mere mortals could not have moved the huge stones into place by hand. They believe that it would have taken giants to complete the immense monuments.

9   Legends of Native Americans provide another source of stories about giants. Some Native Americans believe that the first human beings on earth were a tribe of gigantic Indians. Those Indians were so large that even buffalo seemed tiny next to them. One giant could easily lift a buffalo, throw it over his shoulder, and carry it back to camp. It is said that even a year-old buffalo calf was so small to those giant humans that they could hang the calves from their belts, the way hunters today might carry rabbits.

10   According to legend, the giant Indians did as they pleased. They paid no attention to the Great Spirit. Their disregard made the Great Spirit so angry that he decided to punish them. He caused the rivers, lakes, and seas to overflow, turning the land to mud. The giants were so heavy that they sank into the wet earth and drowned. Some Native Americans claim that the massive bones of the giants can be seen even today. They are the boulders and rocks of the North American countryside.

11   Viking myths of ancient Sweden, Norway, and Denmark tell of yet another breed of giants. According to the myths,

the first living creature was a terrible giant named Ymir. Ymir was slain by Buri, one of the earliest gods. Buri then used Ymir's body to make the earth. The giant's blood formed the seas and lakes. His flesh became the soil. Clouds were made from his brains, and the mountains were formed from his bones. Ymir's hair became the growing things of the earth, and the dome of his skull became the sky.

12   In addition to explaining the part giants played in the beginning of the world, Viking myths tell of the giants' role in the end of the world. The myths predict that one day giants will enter into a long and terrible struggle with the gods. The fight will lead to chaos. Finally, after three terrible winters in a row, there will come a day of doom in which the entire universe will be destroyed. The seas will boil, earthquakes will rip through the land, and as all the forces of evil are turned loose, the dead will rise from their graves. The newly-risen dead will join the giants and monsters of land and sea in a final battle against the gods. Only four gods and two humans will survive. After the battle, the earth will slowly rise again from beneath the waters. On that fresh green earth the two humans, a man and a woman, will start a new family. Slowly they will rebuild the land and create a new world.

13   Did giants really exist? If they did, were they the giants of the myths and

legends? Well, there have always been some people who have grown far above the normal height and size of other human beings. But there is no physical evidence that there were ever entire races of giants. Some of the myths and legends grew up from people's efforts to explain things—such as the beginning of the earth and the building of the pyramids—for which they had no scientific explanation. Others were born when the huge skeletons of monsters from the past—dinosaurs and other huge now extinct beasts—were discovered, before there was scientific knowledge of such creatures. So, yes, there have been and still are, giants of a sort. But the powerful and colorful giants of myth and legend lived mainly in the land of imagination. 🍂

If you have been timed while reading this article, enter your reading time below. Then turn to the Words-per-Minute Table on page 133 and look up your reading speed (words per minute). Enter your reading speed on the graph on page 134.

Reading Time: Lesson 11

_____ : _____
Minutes   Seconds

A | Finding the Main Idea

One statement below expresses the main idea of the article. One statement is too general, or too broad. The other statement explains only part of the article; it is too narrow. Label the statements using the following key:

M—Main Idea   B—Too Broad   N—Too Narrow

_____ 1. The Bible is the source of some of the most famous giant stories, including the stories of Goliath and of Og, the king of Bashan.

_____ 2. Giants have lived in the myths and legends of almost all the earth's cultures, and most came about as a way of explaining otherwise unexplainable phenomena.

_____ 3. The idea of giants has fascinated people for thousands of years.

_____ Score 15 points for a correct M answer.

_____ Score 5 points for each correct B or N answer.

_____ **Total Score:** Finding the Main Idea

B | Recalling Facts

How well do you remember the facts in the article? Put an X in the box next to the answer that correctly completes each statement about the article.

1. Goliath was a
   ☐ a. Palestinian.
   ☐ b. Philistine.
   ☐ c. Philippian.

2. The Biblical giant Og
   ☐ a. slept on the roof of Noah's ark.
   ☐ b. killed Moses.
   ☐ c. was killed by a young shepherd named David.

3. Some Greeks believed that the existence of giants called Cyclopes was proved by what was actually the
   ☐ a. skull of a cyclops.
   ☐ b. rocks and boulders of the countryside.
   ☐ c. skull of an elephant.

4. According to legend, the giant Indians of North America were punished because they
   ☐ a. hung buffalo calves from their belts.
   ☐ b. were so heavy they sank into the mud.
   ☐ c. ignored the Great Spirit.

5. According to Viking legend, at the time of the final disaster, the dead will rise and do battle with the
   ☐ a. giants.
   ☐ b. monsters of land and sea.
   ☐ c. gods.

Score 5 points for each correct answer.

_____ **Total Score:** Recalling Facts

C | Making Inferences

When you combine your own experience and information from a text to draw a conclusion that is not directly stated in that text, you are making an inference. Below are five statements that may or may not be inferences based on information in the article. Label the statements using the following key:

C—Correct Inference   **F—Faulty Inference**

_____ 1. It is almost certain that the pyramids were built by a race of giants.

_____ 2. Most Greeks still do not know anything about elephants.

_____ 3. The Viking myths about giants and the part they will play in the end of the world are taken from the Bible.

_____ 4. People believed less and less in giants as scientific knowledge developed.

_____ 5. Ymir was the largest of the mythological giants.

Score 5 points for each correct answer.

_____ **Total Score:** Making Inferences

D | Using Words Precisely

Each numbered sentence below contains an underlined word or phrase from the article. Following the sentence are three definitions. One definition is closest to the meaning of the underlined word. One definition is opposite or nearly opposite. Label those two definitions using the following key. Do not label the remaining definition.

C—Closest   **O—Opposite or Nearly Opposite**

1. When Goliath and David underlined confronted each other, the young shepherd picked up a small, smooth stone.

    _____ a. faced

    _____ b. turned away from

    _____ c. killed

2. It was logical for the Greeks to assume that the opening in the skull was the socket of a one-eyed giant human.

    _____ a. sensible

    _____ b. scary

    _____ c. unreasonable

3. He became so entangled in his burden, however, that Moses was able to kill him.

    _____ a. excited about

    _____ b. freed from

    _____ c. trapped in

4. They paid no attention to the Great Spirit. Their disregard made the Great Spirit so angry that he decided to punish them.

    _____ a. disrespect

    _____ b. attentiveness

    _____ c. crimes

5. Even today, the Indians point out, the <u>massive</u> bones of the giants can be found in the huge boulders and rocks of the North American countryside.

_____ a. small

_____ b. broken

_____ c. tremendous

_____ Score 3 points for each correct C answer.

_____ Score 2 points for each correct O answer.

_____ **Total Score:** Using Words Precisely

Enter the four total scores in the spaces below, and add them together to find your Reading Comprehension Score. Then record your score on the graph on page 135.

Score	Question Type	Lesson 11
_____	Finding the Main Idea	
_____	Recalling Facts	
_____	Making Inferences	
_____	Using Words Precisely	
_____	**Reading Comprehension Score**	

Author's Approach

Put an X in the box next to the correct answer.

1. The author uses the first sentence of the article to
   □ a. inform the reader about ancient beliefs in giants.
   □ b. try to convince the reader that giants existed thousands of years ago.
   □ c. entertain the reader with a story about giants.

2. Choose the statement below that is the weakest argument for believing that races of giants once existed.
   □ a. There have always been some people who have grown much taller than the normal height and size of other human beings.
   □ b. People have been telling stories about giants since ancient times.
   □ c. Skeletons of huge, extinct beasts have been found, so it seems logical to believe that there were also giant humans.

3. What does the author imply by saying "[Og] roasted the fish by holding them up to the sun"?
   □ a. Og was so tall that he could reach up and hold the fish close enough to the sun to cook them.
   □ b. In ancient times, people didn't have ovens to cook with.
   □ c. Og ate a lot of fish.

4. The author tells this story mainly by
   □ a. comparing myths about the beginning of the earth.
   □ b. using his or her imagination and creativity.
   □ c. telling different stories about giants.

_____ Number of correct answers

Record your personal assessment of your work on the Critical Thinking Chart on page 136.

Summarizing and Paraphrasing

Put an X in the box next to the correct answer.

1. Below are summaries of the article. Choose the summary that says all the most important things about the article but in the fewest words.

☐ a. Since ancient times, people of many cultures have believed that giants once roamed the earth. They offer several types of evidence to explain their beliefs.

☐ b. Goliath was a giant who was defeated by a normal-sized young man named David. People who believe in the Bible point to this story to prove the existence of giants on the earth.

☐ c. The Bible contains several stories of giants, including the story of Goliath. Giants also appear in the myths of various cultures. The ancient Greeks, for instance, believed in a race of giants called the Cyclopes. The Vikings believed that a giant's body was used to make the earth.

2. Choose the sentence that correctly restates the following sentence from the article:

"When a young Hebrew shepherd named David set out to fight the fierce giant, it seemed certain that Goliath would win."

☐ a. When David decided to fight Goliath, most people thought that David would win.

☐ b. When the young shepherd set out to fight David, everyone thought that Goliath would win.

☐ c. When David prepared to fight Goliath, it seemed obvious that the giant would win.

_____ Number of correct answers

Record your personal assessment of your work on the Critical Thinking Chart on page 136.

Critical Thinking

Follow the directions provided for questions 1 and 3. Put an X in the box next to the correct answer for the other questions.

1. For each statement below, write O if it expresses an opinion and write F if it expresses a fact.

_____ a. The great pyramids of Egypt and the Sphinx were built over four thousand years ago.

_____ b. There were no elephants in ancient Greece.

_____ c. Believing in giants is ridiculous.

2. Judging from Og's actions as described in this article, you can predict that he was

☐ a. meek and mild.

☐ b. strong and violent.

☐ c. cruel and evil.

3. Choose from the letters below to correctly complete the following statement. Write the letters on the lines.

In the article, _____ and _____ are alike.

a. the role the Cyclopes played in the creation of the earth according to Greek myths

b. the role giants played in the creation of the earth according to Viking myths

c. the role giants played in the creation of the earth according to Native American legends

4. What was the effect of the giant Indians' disregard for the Great Spirit?

☐ a. The giant Indians could easily lift a buffalo.

☐ b. The giant Indians did as they pleased.

☐ c. The Great Spirit made the rivers, lakes, and seas overflow.

5. What did you have to do to answer question 3?

☐ a. find an effect (something that happened)

☐ b. find a comparison (how things are the same)

☐ c. draw a conclusion (a sensible statement based on the text and your experience)

_____ Number of correct answers

Record your personal assessment of your work on the Critical Thinking Chart on page 136.

Self-Assessment

From reading this article, I have learned

_____

_____

_____

_____

Personal Response

If you could ask the author of the article one question, what would it be?

_____

_____

_____

_____

NESSIE
The Loch Ness Monster

The monster said to be living in the waters of Loch Ness in Scotland is not very scary. Nessie, as she is known, does not attack people. She does not destroy property. She does not try to frighten anyone. In fact, she is quite shy. Usually she goes about her own business and avoids humans. For that reason, most people are not afraid of her. But they are curious. They are incredibly curious. People find Nessie so intriguing that thousands of tourists journey to the Highlands of Scotland each year in hopes of seeing her.

2   Although Nessie now spends most of her time in hiding, she was not always so shy. According to legend, the Loch Ness Monster was once a hostile beast. In 565 A.D., a priest now known as Saint Columba had a very close call with it. He was traveling through Scotland teaching the Christian religion. When he reached the shores of a lake called Loch Ness, he found a funeral in progress. The dead person, he was told, had been killed by the savage bite of a creature living in the lake.

Is the Loch Ness monster a descendant of the plesiosaur, an overgrown seal or otter, or a product of people's imaginations? Plesiosaurs like those pictured here lived in the oceans about 70 million years ago.

3 Though the news disturbed him, Columba was determined to cross the lake. He wanted to take his religion to the people living on the other side. Columba asked his servant to wade into the water to get a boat that was nearby. Perhaps the man's splashing disturbed the monster, for suddenly the creature rose from the water. With a menacing roar, Nessie swam straight for the poor servant. Columba rushed forward, his hand raised. Making the sign of the cross in the air, he cried out, "Think not to go further, nor touch thou that man. Quick! Go back!" According to the man who wrote Columba's biography, the monster withdrew as if "dragged by cords."

4 After her meeting with Saint Columba, Nessie retreated into the depths of Loch Ness. Local folks still caught an occasional glimpse of the monster, but she no longer bothered anybody. In fact she stayed pretty much out of sight until 1933. In that year, a new highway was built next to the lake. During construction, a great deal of dynamite was used to blast through rock. It may have been the noise of the blasting that disturbed Nessie. Or perhaps she was stirred by the boulders that the workmen pushed into the water. In any event, as soon as the highway was opened, Nessie began to appear more often.

5 Two of the first people to see her at that time were Mr. and Mrs. George Spicer of London. They were traveling on the newly built highway when Nessie crossed the road ahead of them. It was broad daylight. What was their reaction to the incredible sight? "It was simply horrible," said Mr. Spicer. Mrs. Spicer described Nessie as "a giant snail with a long neck."

6 Since 1933, around nine thousand sightings have been reported. Nessie has been seen both on land and in the water. Sometimes she appears when the area is almost deserted. But other times she surfaces in full view of many witnesses. Once she showed herself when a bus carrying 27 passengers was passing by. All the people aboard the bus reported that they watched the monster swim for some time. In his book *The Monsters of Loch Ness*, Roy P. Mackal reports 254 detailed eyewitness accounts of sightings of Nessie in the water. He also describes 18 incidents in which Nessie was seen thrashing around on the shores of Loch Ness.

7 Many people have tried to photograph Nessie. The most famous picture ever captured of her was taken by a surgeon named H. K. Wilson. Known as the "surgeon's photo," the picture appeared on the front page of a London newspaper, *The Daily Mail*, in 1934. It shows Nessie with a long, thick neck shaped somewhat like an elephant's trunk. Her head is small and flat on top, like the head of a snake. And her huge barrel-shaped body sports a 25-foot tail.

8 While many people have tried to capture proof of Nessie with a camera (and a number have succeeded in getting pictures much like the surgeon's photo), others have used more complex equipment. Telescopes, binoculars, and movie and television cameras have all been used to look for her. A helicopter and two mini-submarines have hunted her. Sonar has

An alleged photograph of the Loch Ness Monster taken in 1934. Do you see any similarities between this photo and the image on page 108?

also been used to try to detect her presence. Sonar is a device used to locate underwater objects by bouncing sound waves off them.

9   Some scientists think that all those efforts have been successful. They say that the sonar results indicate that a large animal is swimming deep in Loch Ness. They also believe that the many photographs and films of Nessie show that she exists. Many pictures show a creature stirring up the water and leaving a trail of waves as it moves along. The scientists argue that such wave patterns could be created only by a huge creature.

10   Not all scientists, however, are convinced that Nessie is real. Some think that the sonar results proved nothing. Many believe that the creatures in the photographs are simply seals or otters. Others claim that the objects seen in the water are merely sticks or logs.

11   Part of the reason for all the disagreement is that Nessie is terribly shy. Because she hides from people, it is difficult to observe her. But the confusion is not all her fault. Part of the trouble lies with Loch Ness itself. The lake is very large. It is 24 and a half miles long. Some sections are more than 920 feet deep. The water is dark and murky, and its average temperature is only 42 degrees Fahrenheit. The murkiness is caused by peat, which is created by rotting moss and other plants. In Loch Ness the peat is so thick that it is possible to see only to a depth of about 10 feet. In addition, the banks of the lake are very steep—almost vertical. Such conditions make photography almost impossible.

12   While the size of Loch Ness hinders observers, it is ideal for Nessie. Six rivers that flow into Loch Ness bring with them enough fish to feed many monsters. It is estimated that the lake contains 30 million large salmon, plus trout, large pike, and char. It also houses tons of fat, juicy eels. Given all that food, chances are that Nessie never goes hungry.

13   Although the idea of a fish-eating monster may seem a bit strange, there was once a whole group of large creatures that lived on fish. They were dinosaurs called plesiosaurs. They lived in the oceans 65 to 70 million years ago. Some people think that Nessie is a descendant of those dinosaurs. It is possible that plesiosaurs got into Loch Ness when it was still part of the Atlantic Ocean. When land later enclosed the lake, the creatures may have gotten trapped there. If Nessie is descended from the plesiosaurs, she may be a member of a whole family of similar creatures living in the waters of Loch Ness.

14   And speaking of families, Nessie may even have relatives in other parts of the world. Australia has a Nessie-like creature that has been seen in several lakes and rivers. The rivers of Africa, too, contain animals whose descriptions make them sound like first cousins of Nessie. North America also has its Nessie look-alikes. Two lakes in Canada have their own versions of Nessie, and Lake Champlain is home to a monster called Champ. United States monsters also include one that has been spotted in Arkansas's White River. And one in Chesapeake Bay has a name similar to Nessie's. Her name, as you may have guessed, is Chessie.

If you have been timed while reading this article, enter your reading time below. Then turn to the Words-per-Minute Table on page 133 and look up your reading speed (words per minute). Enter your reading speed on the graph on page 134.

Reading Time: Lesson 12

_____ : _____
Minutes   Seconds

A Finding the Main Idea

One statement below expresses the main idea of the article. One statement is too general, or too broad. The other statement explains only part of the article; it is too narrow. Label the statements using the following key:

M—Main Idea   **B—Too Broad**   **N—Too Narrow**

_____ 1. It is possible that a sea-creature ancestor of Nessie got trapped in Loch Ness when it got closed off from the Atlantic Ocean.

_____ 2. People have been trying to determine for hundreds of years whether there really is a Loch Ness monster, and there is some evidence for its existence.

_____ 3. The question of whether or not a monster really exists in Loch Ness has fascinated people for a very long time.

_____ Score 15 points for a correct M answer.

_____ Score 5 points for each correct B or N answer.

_____ **Total Score:** Finding the Main Idea

B Recalling Facts

How well do you remember the facts in the article? Put an X in the box next to the answer that correctly completes each statement about the article.

1. Saint Columba had gone to the Highlands of Scotland to

☐ a. attend the funeral of a man killed by Nessie.

☐ b. convert the Scots to Christianity.

☐ c. fish in the waters of Loch Ness.

2. The fish in Loch Ness

☐ a. were trapped in it when the lake was cut off from the ocean.

☐ b. come in on the rivers that flow into the loch.

☐ c. have died out since the roadway alongside the loch opened in 1933.

3. Mrs. Spicer, who saw Nessie crossing the road in broad daylight, said the monster resembled

☐ a. a snake.

☐ b. the surgeon's photo.

☐ c. a giant snail.

4. The most famous picture of Nessie was taken

☐ a. by a doctor.

☐ b. with sonar.

☐ c. from a mini-submarine.

5. Some scientists think that Nessie may be some sort of

☐ a. brontosaurus.

☐ b. pachyderm.

☐ c. plesiosaur.

Score 5 points for each correct answer.

_____ **Total Score:** Recalling Facts

C Making Inferences

When you combine your own experience and information from a text to draw a conclusion that is not directly stated in that text, you are making an inference. Below are five statements that may or may not be inferences based on information in the article. Label the statements using the following key:

C—Correct Inference   **F—Faulty Inference**

_____ 1. Saint Columba was made a saint because of the miraculous way in which he handled Nessie.

_____ 2. People are still watching for proof of Nessie's existence.

_____ 3. Nessie enjoys the attention of the people who visit Loch Ness to look for her.

_____ 4. There may still be creatures living on the earth that no one knows anything about.

_____ 5. Nessie herself is thought to have swum into the loch in some past age.

Score 5 points for each correct answer.

_____ **Total Score:** Making Inferences

D Using Words Precisely

Each numbered sentence below contains an underlined word or phrase from the article. Following the sentence are three definitions. One definition is closest to the meaning of the underlined word. One definition is opposite or nearly opposite. Label those two definitions using the following key. Do not label the remaining definition.

C—Closest   **O—Opposite or Nearly Opposite**

1. People find Nessie so intriguing that thousands of tourists journey to the Highlands of Scotland each year in hopes of seeing her.

_____ a. shy

_____ b. fascinating

_____ c. uninteresting

2. The dead person, he was told, had been killed by the savage bite of a creature living in the lake.

_____ a. tender

_____ b. vicious

_____ c. accidental

3. With a menacing roar, Nessie swam straight for the poor servant.

_____ a. reassuring

_____ b. echoing

_____ c. threatening

4. After her meeting with Saint Columba, Nessie retreated into the depths of Loch Ness.

_____ a. withdrew

_____ b. moved forward

_____ c. drowned

5. While the size of Loch Ness <u>hinders</u> observers, it is ideal for Nessie.

_____ a. helps

_____ b. terrifies

_____ c. makes things difficult for

_____ Score 3 points for each correct C answer.

_____ Score 2 points for each correct O answer.

_____ **Total Score:** Using Words Precisely

Enter the four total scores in the spaces below, and add them together to find your Reading Comprehension Score. Then record your score on the graph on page 135.

Score	Question Type	Lesson 12
_____	Finding the Main Idea	
_____	Recalling Facts	
_____	Making Inferences	
_____	Using Words Precisely	
_____	**Reading Comprehension Score**	

Author's Approach

Put an X in the box next to the correct answer.

1. The author probably wrote this article in order to

☐ a. convince the reader that Nessie exists.

☐ b. convince the reader that Nessie doesn't exist.

☐ c. tell the reader about the monster that may be living in Loch Ness.

2. How is the author's purpose for writing the article expressed in paragraph 13?

☐ a. The author informs the reader about Nessie's possible relation to the plesiosaurs.

☐ b. The author claims that Nessie is a descendant of the plesiosaurs.

☐ c. The author points out that the idea of a fish-eating monster is ridiculous.

3. Choose the statement below that best explains how the author addresses the opposing point of view in the article.

☐ a. To convince those who doubt that Nessie is real, the author cites eyewitness evidence and the results of sonar tests in Loch Ness.

☐ b. To convince those who doubt that Nessie is real, the author refers to scientists who believe that the creatures in the photographs are seals or otters.

☐ c. To convince those who doubt that Nessie is real, the author relates a legend involving Saint Columba and the monster.

_____ Number of correct answers

Record your personal assessment of your work on the Critical Thinking Chart on page 136.

CRITICAL THINKING

Summarizing and Paraphrasing

Follow the directions provided for questions 1 and 2. Put an X in the box next to the correct answer for question 3.

1. Look for the important ideas and events in paragraphs 2 and 3. Summarize those paragraphs in one or two sentences.

_____

_____

_____

2. Reread paragraph 7 in the article. Below, write a summary of the paragraph in no more than 25 words.

_____

_____

_____

_____

Reread your summary and decide whether it covers the important ideas in the paragraph. Next, decide how to shorten the summary to 15 words or less without leaving out any essential information. Write this summary below.

_____

_____

_____

3. Choose the sentence that correctly restates the following sentence from the article:

"While many people have tried to capture proof of Nessie with a camera (and a number have succeeded in getting pictures much like the surgeon's photo), others have used more complex equipment."

☐ a. Although many people have tried to capture Nessie, most have just been able to take pictures of her.

☐ b. While some people have taken pictures of Nessie, others have used more complicated equipment to prove that she exists.

☐ c. While many people have taken pictures of the surgeon's photo, others have used more complicated equipment to prove Nessie's existence.

_____ Number of correct answers

Record your personal assessment of your work on the Critical Thinking Chart on page 136.

Critical Thinking

Put an X in the box next to the correct answer for questions 1 and 2. Follow the directions provided for the other questions.

1. Which of the following statements from the article is an opinion rather than a fact?

☐ a. "Sonar is a device used to locate underwater objects by bouncing sound waves off them."

☐ b. "[Plesiosaurs] lived in the oceans 65 to 70 million years ago."

☐ c. "'It [the monster] was simply horrible.'"

2. From what the article told about Nessie and the tourists who come to see her, you can predict that

☐ a. the monster will continue to hide from the tourists.

☐ b. one day the monster will attack a tourist who tries to get too close to her.

☐ c. a tourist will try to kill the monster.

3. Using what is told about Nessie and plesiosaurs in the article, name three ways Nessie is similar to and three ways Nessie is different from a plesiosaur. Cite the paragraph number(s) where you found details in the article to support your conclusions.

Similarities

_____

_____

_____

Differences

_____

_____

_____

4. Read paragraph 11. Then choose from the letters below to correctly complete the following statement. Write the letters on the lines.

According to paragraph 11, _____ because _____.

a. the water of Loch Ness is very dark and murky

b. the water temperature in Loch Ness is only 42 degrees Fahrenheit

c. Nessie is hard to see

_____ Number of correct answers

Record your personal assessment of your work on the Critical Thinking Chart on page 136.

Personal Response

This article is different from other articles about monsters I've read because

_____

_____

and Nessie is unlike other monsters because

_____

_____

Self-Assessment

Which concepts or ideas from the article were difficult to understand?

_____

_____

Which were easy to understand?

_____

_____

CRITICAL THINKING

MYSTERY CATS

While cougars (left) are not native to England, many people believe that some kind of wild, cougar-like cat is attacking livestock in parts of the country.

Something is terrorizing the countryside in southern England. For years, farmers there have told of a strange creature that roams the moors and meadows. Often, in the dead of night, this creature attacks farms, killing sheep, goats, and calves. Many people have tried to capture it; none have succeeded. And so the beast lives on, traveling freely, eluding humans, leaving death and destruction in its wake.

2   Most people agree that there is not one beast, but rather a whole family of these creatures. They have been spotted in many places throughout a region covering roughly 10,000 square miles. The first sightings occurred in 1963, when residents of Surrey, England, began seeing animals that looked like house cats but were much, much bigger. The creatures were jet-black, about three feet long, with long, bushy tails, pointed ears, and a loping gait. Some people noticed the creatures slinking around farms; others heard their eerie cries. Still others saw and heard nothing but later discovered that their farm animals had been ruthlessly

attacked and killed by the prowling menace.

3   Since 1963, these fierce creatures have been seen countless times across southern England. In Exmoor, Dartmoor, and Bodmin, residents have taken to calling this animal "the Beast." In other parts of England, people refer to the creatures simply as "mystery cats."

4   Some people have suggested that these real-life monsters are actually pumas, or panthers. The description of the monsters certainly seems to fit that of the powerful cats. But there are no pumas in England; the species is not native to the British Isles. The only pumas to be found in the area are ones that live in zoos.

5   Other people claim that the animals are not cats at all, but rather wild dogs. Their paw prints are more like those of big dogs than those of cats. But eyewitnesses insist that the animals are not dogs. "It was the size of a big dog," declared one man, "but more of a cat's body." Besides, dogs tend to kill by biting at the hind legs. These creatures go straight for their victims' throats.

6   Several efforts have been made to capture a mystery cat for study and identification. In 1983, farmers in Exmoor found themselves at the mercy of the creature. Again and again they awoke to find their livestock ripped apart. The government sent in the Royal Marines in an effort to find the "Beast of Exmoor." They combed the area, hoping to capture at least one specimen, but their efforts turned up nothing. The wily cats did not show themselves while the Marines were around.

7   In the 1990s, the government tried again. They sent wildlife experts out in search of the "Beast of Bodmin." The scientists examined a six-inch paw print on a farm near Cornwall. They studied photographs taken by local residents. They checked out bite marks on animals that had survived attacks. But they never saw the Beast. Finally the scientists concluded that the creature did not exist. They said that most of the evidence they examined could be attributed to attacks made by domestic cats and dogs.

8   Farmer John Goodenough was furious when he heard about this official report. After all, it did not explain how and why so many farm animals were being viciously killed. Goodenough himself has lost 10 ewes and 3 calves in the last few years. He is sure that the Beast is out there and that it poses an increasing threat to farmers throughout the region. In his opinion, the number of mystery cats is increasing rapidly. "We are in one hell of a position now," he told one reporter, "because they are breeding fast."

9   Goodenough is not the only one who still believes in the Beast. Every year, more and more people have encounters with it. David Bryne had never been convinced of the creature's existence—until he saw one

What kind of cat is it that is causing so much destruction in the peaceful English countryside?

for himself. Bryne and his wife were driving down the road one night. Suddenly they spotted a huge, black, catlike creature. "It was just freaky," Bryne told reporters the next day. "I was a nonbeliever until last night."

10   Stephen Challis saw a big black beast in a field on September 1, 1995. Jim Turnbull saw a similar creature from his porch two nights later. He described it as "about three times the size of a domestic cat and about two feet tall." Soon after seeing it, he said, he heard a growling sound like that made by a leopard.

11   Policeman Richard Hunt also saw the mystery cat with his own eyes. In fact, he managed to capture the beast on video-tape. Hunt was on vacation in Cornwall. There, on July 19, 1996, he spotted an enormous cat crossing the dunes just 300 yards away. Luckily, he had his video camera with him. The resulting film shows a giant catlike animal loping through the grass.

12   Seeing a mystery cat may be exciting, but seeing the damage it does is down-right frightening. In December 1994, Ron Kirby saw one of these monsters maul and kill a small deer just 100 yards from his home. In January 1996, a Beast struck in

Essex. It left behind seven sheep and one goat, all with their throats ripped out.

13   And now there is evidence that these predators may be broadening their attacks. On January 23, 1997, Madelaine Dinsmore found the bumper of her Range Rover chewed to pieces in Brooksman Park, Hertfordshire. She believes it was the work of a mystery cat. Could this be a sign of things to come? Is it possible that the Beasts will someday embark on a new killing campaign, this one aimed not at livestock but at humans? 🍃

If you have been timed while reading this article, enter your reading time below. Then turn to the Words-per-Minute Table on page 133 and look up your reading speed (words per minute). Enter your reading speed on the graph on page 134.

Reading Time: **Lesson 13**

_____ : _____

Minutes   Seconds

A **Finding the Main Idea**

One statement below expresses the main idea of the article. One statement is too general, or too broad. The other statement explains only part of the article; it is too narrow. Label the statements using the following key:

M—Main Idea   **B—Too Broad**   **N—Too Narrow**

_____ 1. A mystery cat attacked and killed several of John Goodenough's livestock.

_____ 2. A mysterious creature is causing fear and death in the English countryside.

_____ 3. For many years, mysterious catlike beasts have been attacking livestock and frightening the residents of the countryside in southern England.

_____ Score 15 points for a correct M answer.

_____ Score 5 points for each correct B or N answer.

_____ **Total Score:** Finding the Main Idea

B **Recalling Facts**

How well do you remember the facts in the article? Put an X in the box next to the answer that correctly completes each statement about the article.

1. The first sightings of the strange creatures occurred in 1963 in
   - ☐ a. Bodmin, England.
   - ☐ b. Surrey, England.
   - ☐ c. Exmoor, England.

2. The description of the mystery cat is similar to that of a
   - ☐ a. panther.
   - ☐ b. wild dog.
   - ☐ c. domestic dog.

3. A mystery cat tends to kill livestock by
   - ☐ a. going straight for the throat.
   - ☐ b. biting at the hind legs.
   - ☐ c. crushing animals with its paws.

4. Wildlife experts searching for the "Beast of Bodmin" concluded that the
   - ☐ a. Beast poses an increasing threat to farmers throughout the region.
   - ☐ b. attacks on animals in the area were probably caused by domestic cats and dogs.
   - ☐ c. mystery cats are breeding fast.

5. On January 23, 1997, Madelaine Dinsmore
   - ☐ a. heard a growling sound like that made by a leopard.
   - ☐ b. saw a mystery cat kill a small deer.
   - ☐ c. discovered that her car bumper had been chewed to pieces.

Score 5 points for each correct answer.

_____ **Total Score:** Recalling Facts

C Making Inferences

When you combine your own experience and information from a text to draw a conclusion that is not directly stated in that text, you are making an inference. Below are five statements that may or may not be inferences based on information in the article. Label the statements using the following key:

C—Correct Inference   F—Faulty Inference

_____ 1. So far, the mystery cats have tried to avoid humans.

_____ 2. Wild cats kill by biting and tearing at their victims' throats.

_____ 3. If the mystery cats continue to breed, more and more livestock animals will be killed in southern England.

_____ 4. There is no hard evidence that anything is really killing livestock in England.

_____ 5. Most farmers in southern England agree with the government and believe that the mystery cats do not exist.

> Score 5 points for each correct answer.
>
> _____ **Total Score:** Making Inferences

D Using Words Precisely

Each numbered sentence below contains an underlined word or phrase from the article. Following the sentence are three definitions. One definition is closest to the meaning of the underlined word. One definition is opposite or nearly opposite. Label those two definitions using the following key. Do not label the remaining definition.

C—Closest   O—Opposite or Nearly Opposite

1. And so the beast lives on, traveling freely, <u>eluding</u> humans, leaving death and destruction in its wake.

    _____ a. angering

    _____ b. confronting

    _____ c. dodging

2. Still others saw and heard nothing but later discovered that their farm animals had been <u>ruthlessly</u> attacked and killed by the prowling menace.

    _____ a. viciously

    _____ b. gently

    _____ c. probably

3. The resulting film shows a giant catlike animal <u>loping</u> through the grass.

    _____ a. standing still

    _____ b. jogging

    _____ c. eating

4. And now there is evidence that these <u>predators</u> may be broadening their attacks.

_____ a. victims

_____ b. farmers

_____ c. hunters

5. Is it possible that the Beasts will someday <u>embark on</u> a new killing campaign, this one aimed not at livestock but at humans?

_____ a. observe

_____ b. begin

_____ c. end

_____ Score 3 points for each correct C answer.

_____ Score 2 points for each correct O answer.

_____ **Total Score:** Using Words Precisely

Enter the four total scores in the spaces below, and add them together to find your Reading Comprehension Score. Then record your score on the graph on page 135.

Score	Question Type	Lesson 13
_____	Finding the Main Idea	
_____	Recalling Facts	
_____	Making Inferences	
_____	Using Words Precisely	
_____	**Reading Comprehension Score**	

Author's Approach

Put an X in the box next to the correct answer.

1. What is the author's purpose in writing "Mystery Cats"?

☐ a. To convey a mood of terror

☐ b. To inform the reader about the creatures that are killing livestock in southern England

☐ c. To compare wild cats with wild dogs

2. How is the author's purpose for writing the article expressed in paragraph 13?

☐ a. The author tries to inspire fear by suggesting that the beasts may begin attacking cars.

☐ b. The author tells the reader that the beasts may no longer be limiting their attacks to livestock.

☐ c. The author tries to convince the reader that the attack on the vehicle was committed by a mystery cat.

3. From the statement "The wily cats did not show themselves while the Marines were around," you can conclude that the author wants the reader to think that

☐ a. the Marines didn't try very hard to find the mystery cats.

☐ b. whatever creatures were killing livestock were smart enough to hide from the Marines.

☐ c. the frightened creatures had left the region.

_____ Number of correct answers

Record your personal assessment of your work on the Critical Thinking Chart on page 136.

CRITICAL THINKING

Summarizing and Paraphrasing

Follow the directions provided for question 1. Put an X in the box next to the correct answer for question 2.

1. Reread paragraph 6 in the article. Below, write a summary of the paragraph in no more than 25 words.

_____

_____

_____

Reread your summary and decide whether it covers the important ideas in the paragraph. Next, decide how to shorten the summary to 15 words or less without leaving out any essential information. Write this summary below.

_____

_____

_____

2. Read the statement about the article below. Then read the paraphrase of that statement. Choose the reason that best tells why the paraphrase does not say the same thing as the statement.

   Statement: Some farmers were furious after government officials decided that the mystery cat didn't exist and that the animal attacks in Bodmin were probably carried out by domestic cats and dogs.

Paraphrase: Government officials concluded that cats and dogs were probably responsible for the attacks in Bodmin.

☐ a. Paraphrase says too much.

☐ b. Paraphrase doesn't say enough.

☐ c. Paraphrase doesn't agree with the statement about the article.

_____ Number of correct answers

Record your personal assessment of your work on the Critical Thinking Chart on page 136.

Critical Thinking

Follow the directions provided for questions 1 and 3. Put an X in the box next to the correct answer for questions 2, 4, and 5.

1. For each statement below, write O if it expresses an opinion and write F if it expresses a fact.

_____ a. It was right for residents to be angry when they heard the government's official report.

_____ b. Pumas are not native to England.

_____ c. No one has been able to capture a mystery cat.

2. From the events in the article, you can predict that the following will happen next:

☐ a. Fewer attacks will occur as the mystery cats die out.

☐ b. The mystery cats will stop attacking animals and begin concentrating on cars.

☐ c. More and more attacks will occur, perhaps even some on humans.

CRITICAL THINKING

3. Choose from the letters below to correctly complete the following statement. Write the letters on the lines.

    According to the article, _____ and _____ are different.

    a.   the paw prints of the mystery cat

    b.   the paw prints of a dog

    c.   the paw prints of a domestic cat

4. What was the cause of the British government's decision to send the Royal Marines to Exmoor in 1983?

    ☐ a.   The Royal Marines were unable to find any mystery cats.

    ☐ b.   The livestock on many farms in Exmoor were being killed by an unknown creature.

    ☐ c.   The Marines studied paw prints and photographs taken by local residents.

5. What did you have to do to answer question 3?

    ☐ a.   find an opinion (what someone thinks about something)

    ☐ b.   draw a conclusion (a sensible statement based on the text and your experience)

    ☐ c.   find a contrast (how things are different)

_____ Number of correct answers

Record your personal assessment of your work on the Critical Thinking Chart on page 136.

Personal Response

What new question do you have about this topic?

_____

_____

_____

_____

Self-Assessment

A word or phrase in the article that I do not understand is

_____

_____

_____

_____

CRITICAL THINKING

THE FLORIDA SKUNK APE

It was a cool February night in 1970. H. C. "Buz" Osborn and four companions were sleeping peacefully in their tents. They were all worn out after a day spent studying a Native American burial ground in southern Florida. Suddenly, at 3 A.M., a noise woke them. Looking up, they saw a strange eight-foot creature standing just outside the flap doors of their tents. It was covered with hair and, according to one of the men, "smelled awful." But the creature did not harm the men, and soon it disappeared into the dark night.

2 In the morning, the campers found five-toed footprints around their tent. The prints were 17½ inches long and 11 inches wide. They must have been made by the massive creature the men had seen the night before. Osborn was a no-nonsense kind of guy. An engineer and amateur archaeologist, he had never believed in the Florida legend about a Skunk Ape living in the remote regions of the Everglades. But, Osborn said, the visitor early that morning and the prints it left behind "made a believer out of me."

The Skunk Ape is Florida's version of Big Foot, or Sasquatch. The arrow points to a figure in the circle that many say proves the Skunk Ape exists. Others believe that it's only a man in a gorilla suit.

3   Osborn and his friends haven't been the only people to notice this odd creature. Since the 1920s, there have been numerous sightings of the so-called Florida Skunk Ape. The descriptions all fit a similar pattern. The Skunk Ape has been reported to be seven or eight feet tall. Most eyewitnesses have guessed that it weighs at least 300 pounds. They agree that its body is covered with black or brown hair. And they all say that the Skunk Ape has a truly offensive odor. It smells like a mixture of rotten eggs, moldy cheese, and goat dung. According to an old legend, it smells this way because it spends most of its time hiding in muddy abandoned alligator caves. It is this stench that gives the creature its name.

4   Similar broad-shouldered, hulking humanoids have been seen in many other parts of the world. There is a hairy fellow named Bigfoot who allegedly roams the high mountains of California. Sasquatch has been sighted in the Pacific Northwest. Then there is the Abominable Snowman, or Yeti, who is said to live in the Himalayas.

5   Could the Florida Skunk Ape be a relative of these mysterious creatures? Could it have survived all these years in the Everglades? If it wanted to hide, of course, the vast swamp wouldn't be a bad place to do it. Before the Civil War, runaway slaves sometimes found refuge in the Everglades. So, too, did the Seminole Indians during their war with the United States. Since the 1920s, however, the Everglades have been shrinking under the pressure of human development. Are there now more Skunk Ape sightings because this creature's habitat is getting smaller?

6   From all accounts, the Skunk Ape is a nice guy—for a monster. There are no reports that it has ever hurt anyone. In fact, it appears to be a vegetarian who likes beans. A popular story is that campers who leave a pot of lima beans outside their tent at night will wake up the next morning to find that the beans are gone.

7   Most sightings of the Florida Skunk Ape have occurred at night or from a considerable distance. Photographs of the creature usually show nothing more than a brown speck in the distant background. In 1997, Vince Doerr, the fire chief of Ochopee, a tiny hamlet in the Everglades, saw something run across a road. "I was riding along when, 800 feet ahead of me, a brown-looking tall thing ran across the road. It wasn't a bear—that's for sure. It ran into the woods." Before it did, however, Doerr took a photo. The print was too vague to tell for sure what it was. "I think it was somebody playing a hoax," said the skeptical Doerr. "I don't know who it is. But this [Skunk Ape] legend has been around here for years."

8   Not everyone agrees that the Skunk Ape is a fake. David Shealy, a longtime

The Skunk Ape roams the swampy land of the Florida Everglades.

resident of the swamp, saw the Skunk Ape when he was a boy. "I believe that there's something out there," he said. "And it's been around for a long time, but it's been hidden." Shealy has studied the reports and photos of the Skunk Ape. "At first, I thought maybe it was an escaped gorilla. But from the photographs, it looks to be six to seven feet tall, and the tallest gorilla is only about five feet."

9   Perhaps, though, Vince Doerr is onto something. Perhaps the Skunk Ape is just a prankster in a gorilla suit. That explanation makes economic sense. A mysterious beast in the Everglades would be good for tourism. However Shealy, a gift shop owner, denies that he is part of a hoax. "This isn't about money. I'm just telling you what I saw and what other people saw."

10   Dow Roland, a tour guide in the Everglades, said that some of his customers started screaming when they spotted an odd creature. "It looked like Bigfoot or someone in a big gorilla suit," reported Roland. But he went on to point out a couple of flaws in the gorilla-suit theory. It is awfully hot in the Everglades. So why would anyone want to run around the swampy area wearing such a hot outfit? Besides, pulling off such a loony stunt could be dangerous. The prankster could get shot.

11   So the legend of the Skunk Ape lives on. Is it for real or just a ploy to draw in tourists? Everyone in the Everglades seems to have an opinion. But one thing is certain—someone in Florida is crazy. Is it all the people who insist that the Skunk Ape really exists? Is it all the people who refuse to accept the evidence that "proves" the Skunk Ape's existence? Or could the only crazy person be some nut running through the woods in a sweaty gorilla suit risking getting shot?

If you have been timed while reading this article, enter your reading time below. Then turn to the Words-per-Minute Table on page 133 and look up your reading speed (words per minute). Enter your reading speed on the graph on page 134.

Reading Time: **Lesson 14**

_____ : _____
Minutes   Seconds

A **Finding the Main Idea**

One statement below expresses the main idea of the article. One statement is too general, or too broad. The other statement explains only part of the article; it is too narrow. Label the statements using the following key:

M—Main Idea   **B—Too Broad**   **N—Too Narrow**

_____ 1. A mysterious creature known as the Skunk Ape is said to inhabit the Florida Everglades.

_____ 2. People have reported seeing mysterious, hairy humanoids in many parts of the world.

_____ 3. The Skunk Ape gets its name from its stench, which has been described as smelling like a mixture of rotten eggs, moldy cheese, and goat dung.

_____ Score 15 points for a correct M answer.

_____ Score 5 points for each correct B or N answer.

_____ **Total Score:** Finding the Main Idea

B **Recalling Facts**

How well do you remember the facts in the article? Put an X in the box next to the answer that correctly completes each statement about the article.

1. H. C. Osborn is
   ☐ a. the fire chief of Ochopee.
   ☐ b. a gift shop owner.
   ☐ c. an amateur archaeologist.

2. According to legend, the Skunk Ape spends much of its time in
   ☐ a. the Himalayas.
   ☐ b. abandoned alligator caves.
   ☐ c. swamp water.

3. In the past, the Everglades was a hiding place for
   ☐ a. Yeti.
   ☐ b. Sasquatch.
   ☐ c. the Seminole Indians.

4. The Skunk Ape is especially fond of eating
   ☐ a. lima beans.
   ☐ b. meat.
   ☐ c. humans.

5. Vince Doerr thinks that the Skunk Ape is
   ☐ a. an escaped gorilla.
   ☐ b. real.
   ☐ c. a prankster in a gorilla suit.

_____ Score 5 points for each correct answer.

_____ **Total Score:** Recalling Facts

C | Making Inferences

When you combine your own experience and information from a text to draw a conclusion that is not directly stated in that text, you are making an inference. Below are five statements that may or may not be inferences based on information in the article. Label the statements using the following key:

C—Correct Inference   **F—Faulty Inference**

_____ 1. The Skunk Ape is a dangerous creature.

_____ 2. The land area covered by the Everglades is smaller now than it was before the Civil War.

_____ 3. The Skunk Ape would never eat a pot of beef stew left outside a tent overnight.

_____ 4. Some people would like to shoot the Skunk Ape.

_____ 5. No one in the Everglades believes that the Skunk Ape really exists.

Score 5 points for each correct answer.

_____ **Total Score:** Making Inferences

D | Using Words Precisely

Each numbered sentence below contains an underlined word or phrase from the article. Following the sentence are three definitions. One definition is closest to the meaning of the underlined word. One definition is opposite or nearly opposite. Label those two definitions using the following key. Do not label the remaining definition.

C—Closest   **O—Opposite or Nearly Opposite**

1. An engineer and <u>amateur</u> archaeologist, he had never believed in the Florida legend about a Skunk Ape living in the remote regions of the Everglades.

_____ a. professional

_____ b. former

_____ c. inexperienced

2. It is this <u>stench</u> that gives the creature its name.

_____ a. legend

_____ b. foul odor

_____ c. sweet perfume

3. Before the Civil War, runaway slaves sometimes found <u>refuge</u> in the Everglades.

_____ a. safe shelter

_____ b. a dangerous place

_____ c. employment

4. But he went on to point out a couple of <u>flaws</u> in the gorilla-suit theory.

_____ a. ideas

_____ b. perfect features

_____ c. defects

5. Besides, pulling off such a <u>loony</u> stunt could be dangerous.

_____ a. sensible

_____ b. crazy

_____ c. popular

_____ Score 3 points for each correct C answer.

_____ Score 2 points for each correct O answer.

_____ **Total Score:** Using Words Precisely

Enter the four total scores in the spaces below, and add them together to find your Reading Comprehension Score. Then record your score on the graph on page 135.

Score	Question Type	Lesson 14
_____	Finding the Main Idea	
_____	Recalling Facts	
_____	Making Inferences	
_____	Using Words Precisely	
_____	**Reading Comprehension Score**	

Author's Approach

Put an X in the box next to the correct answer.

1. Choose the statement below that is the weakest argument for believing that the Skunk Ape is real.

   ☐ a. Many people have seen the Skunk Ape.

   ☐ b. If you put out lima beans, the Skunk Ape's favorite food, at night, they will be gone in the morning.

   ☐ c. Some people have actually taken photographs of the Skunk Ape.

2. What does the author imply by saying "A mysterious beast in the Everglades is good for tourism"?

   ☐ a. The Skunk Ape is probably a tourist dressed up in a gorilla suit.

   ☐ b. Fear of the Skunk Ape would prevent most people from visiting the Everglades.

   ☐ c. People would come to the Everglades just to see the Skunk Ape.

3. Choose the statement below that best describes the author's position in paragraph 11.

   ☐ a. The author believes in the legend of the Skunk Ape.

   ☐ b. The author believes that everyone in the Everglades is crazy.

   ☐ c. The author is not sure whether the Skunk Ape exists or not.

4. The author tells this story mainly by

   ☐ a. describing various sightings and opinions about the Skunk Ape.

   ☐ b. expressing his own opinion about the Skunk Ape.

   ☐ c. retelling H. C. Osborn's experience with the Skunk Ape.

_____ Number of correct answers

Record your personal assessment of your work on the Critical Thinking Chart on page 136.

CRITICAL THINKING

Summarizing and Paraphrasing

Follow the directions provided for questions 1 and 2. Put an X in the box next to the correct answer for question 3.

1. Look for the important ideas and events in paragraphs 1 and 2. Summarize those paragraphs in one or two sentences.

_____

_____

_____

2. Complete the following one-sentence summary of the article using the lettered phrases from the phrase bank below. Write the letters on the lines.

> **Phrase Bank:**
> a. Osborn's encounter with the creature
> b. opinions about whether or not the creature is a fake
> c. what the Skunk Ape looks, smells, and acts like

The article about the Skunk Ape begins with _____, goes on to explain _____, and ends with _____.

3. Choose the best one-sentence paraphrase for the following sentence from the article:
"A popular story is that campers who leave a pot of lima beans outside their tent at night will wake up the next morning to find that the beans are gone."

☐ a. Legend has it that a pot of lima beans left outside a tent at night will be empty the next morning.

☐ b. Legend has it that campers who leave a pot of lima beans outside their tent find that the tent is gone the next morning.

☐ c. Legend has it that campers who leave a pot of lima beans outside their tent are gone the next morning.

> _____ Number of correct answers
>
> Record your personal assessment of your work on the Critical Thinking Chart on page 136.

Critical Thinking

Put an X in the box next to the correct answer for questions 1, 2, and 4. Follow the directions provided for question 3.

1. Which of the following statements from the article is an opinion rather than a fact?

☐ a. "Before the Civil War, runaway slaves sometimes found refuge in the Everglades."

☐ b. "But one thing is certain—someone in Florida is crazy."

☐ c. "Since the 1920s, however, the Everglades have been shrinking under the pressure of human development."

2. From what the article told about the Skunk Ape, you can predict that it would

☐ a. try to kill anyone running around the Everglades in a gorilla suit.

☐ b. not hurt a camper in the Everglades.

☐ c. like to leave the Everglades and live in the Himalayas.

3. Choose from the letters below to correctly complete the following statement. Write the letters on the lines.

   In the article, _____ and _____ are alike.

   a. Vince Doerr's opinion of the Skunk Ape

   b. David Shealy's opinion of the Skunk Ape

   c. H. C. Osborn's opinion of the Skunk Ape

4. What was the cause of the Skunk Ape's smell?

☐ a. It eats a lot of lima beans.

☐ b. It wears a gorilla suit.

☐ c. It hides in alligator caves.

___

_____ Number of correct answers

Record your personal assessment of your work on the Critical Thinking Chart on page 136.

Personal Response

I agree with the author because

_____

_____

_____

_____

Self-Assessment

I can't really understand how

_____

_____

_____

_____

Compare and Contrast

Think about the articles you have read in Unit Two. Pick the four monsters you felt were the most frightening. Write the titles of the articles that described them in the first column of the chart below. Use information you learned from the articles to fill in the empty boxes in the chart.

Title	How does this monster hurt humans or animals?	What makes this monster look frightening?	What qualities or features of this monster make it dangerous?

Imagine that you met this monster tonight. What would you do? Describe in detail how you would react. _____

_____

_____

Words-per-Minute Table

Unit Two

Directions: If you were timed while reading an article, refer to the Reading Time you recorded in the box at the end of the article. Use this words-per-minute table to determine your reading speed for that article. Then plot your reading speed on the graph on page 134.

Lesson	8	9	10	11	12	13	14	
No. of Words	1111	1086	1203	1301	1284	945	992	
1:30	741	724	802	867	856	630	661	**90**
1:40	667	652	722	781	770	567	595	**100**
1:50	606	592	656	710	700	515	541	**110**
2:00	556	543	602	651	642	473	496	**120**
2:10	513	501	555	600	593	436	458	**130**
2:20	476	465	516	558	550	405	425	**140**
2:30	444	434	481	520	514	378	397	**150**
2:40	417	407	451	488	482	354	372	**160**
2:50	392	383	425	459	453	334	350	**170**
3:00	370	362	401	434	428	315	331	**180**
3:10	351	343	380	411	405	298	313	**190**
3:20	333	326	361	390	385	284	298	**200**
3:30	317	310	344	372	367	270	283	**210**
3:40	303	296	328	355	350	258	271	**220**
3:50	290	283	314	339	335	247	259	**230**
4:00	278	272	301	325	321	236	248	**240**
4:10	267	261	289	312	308	227	238	**250**
4:20	256	251	278	300	296	218	229	**260**
4:30	247	241	267	289	285	210	220	**270**
4:40	238	233	258	279	275	203	213	**280**
4:50	230	225	249	269	266	196	205	**290**
5:00	222	217	241	260	257	189	198	**300**
5:10	215	210	233	252	249	183	192	**310**
5:20	208	204	226	244	241	177	186	**320**
5:30	202	198	219	237	233	172	180	**330**
5:40	196	192	212	230	227	167	175	**340**
5:50	190	186	206	223	220	162	170	**350**
6:00	185	181	201	217	214	158	165	**360**
6:10	180	176	195	211	208	153	161	**370**
6:20	175	171	190	205	203	149	157	**380**
6:30	171	167	185	200	198	145	153	**390**
6:40	167	163	180	195	193	142	149	**400**
6:50	163	159	176	190	188	138	145	**410**
7:00	159	155	172	186	183	135	142	**420**
7:10	155	152	168	182	179	132	138	**430**
7:20	152	148	164	177	175	129	135	**440**
7:30	148	145	160	173	171	126	132	**450**
7:40	145	142	157	170	167	123	129	**460**
7:50	142	139	154	166	164	121	127	**470**
8:00	139	136	150	163	161	118	124	**480**

Minutes and Seconds

Seconds

Plotting Your Progress: Reading Speed

Unit Two

Directions: If you were timed while reading an article, write your words-per-minute rate for that article in the box under the number of the lesson. Then plot your reading speed on the graph by putting a small X on the line directly above the number of the lesson, across from the number of words per minute you read. As you mark your speed for each lesson, graph your progress by drawing a line to connect the X's.

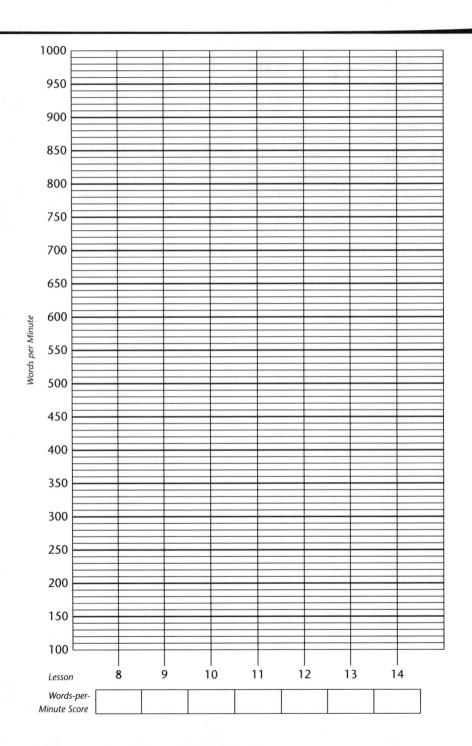

Lesson: 8 9 10 11 12 13 14

Words-per-Minute Score

Plotting Your Progress: Reading Comprehension

Unit Two

Directions: Write your Reading Comprehension score for each lesson in the box under the number of the lesson. Then plot your score on the graph by putting a small X on the line directly above the number of the lesson and across from the score you earned. As you mark your score for each lesson, graph your progress by drawing a line to connect the X's.

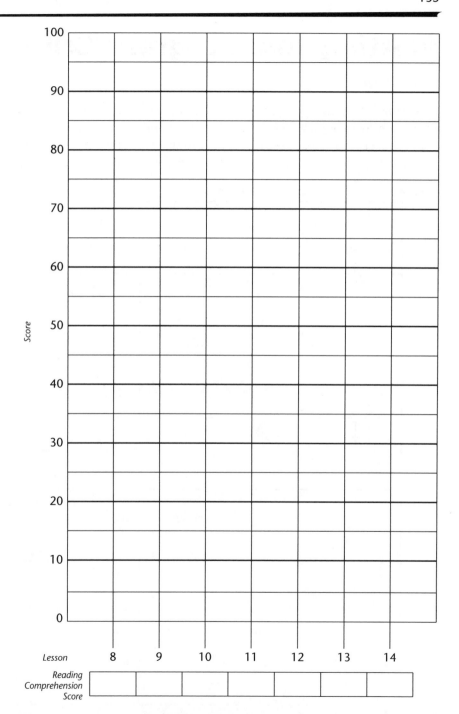

Plotting Your Progress: Critical Thinking

Unit Two

Directions: Work with your teacher to evaluate your responses to the Critical Thinking questions for each lesson. Then fill in the appropriate spaces in the chart below. For each lesson and each type of Critical Thinking question, do the following: Mark a minus sign (–) in the box to indicate areas in which you feel you could improve. Mark a plus sign (+) to indicate areas in which you feel you did well. Mark a minus-slash-plus sign (–/+) to indicate areas in which you had mixed success. Then write any comments you have about your performance, including ideas for improvement.

Lesson	Author's Approach	Summarizing and Paraphrasing	Critical Thinking
8			
9			
10			
11			
12			
13			
14			

UNIT THREE

GRENDEL

Old King Hrothgar should have been a happy man. He and his Viking warriors were the terrors of the European seas. When his brave men attacked a coastal city or a sailing ship, they were almost always victorious. Their robbings and lootings had made them rich, so when they weren't off fighting, Hrothgar and his men lived in splendor in Denmark. They surrounded themselves with plush furs and brilliant ornaments of gold. In the evenings they gathered in the king's great drinking hall to eat, drink, and sing songs. Those celebrations usually ended with everyone collapsing into a long, contented sleep.

2   Despite all the merrymaking, however, King Hrothgar was deeply troubled. For 12 years, a dark and horrifying creature had been terrorizing Hrothgar's kingdom. The creature, whose name was Grendel, was a monster of human shape but of super-human size and strength. Each night the beast dragged himself out of the swamp where he lived, and attacked the local villagers. Often when Hrothgar's warriors awoke from their sleep, they found the

Several years after Beowulf kills Grendel, he returns to his own country and battles a dragon. In this fight, Beowulf is mortally wounded.

doors of the drinking hall bashed in and several of their companions missing. The king ordered the doors strengthened with iron bands, but it did no good. Grendel's murderous raids continued.

3   Finally, in desperation, the Vikings decided to lay a trap for the monster. One night, a group of warriors stationed themselves as guards outside the king's drinking hall. They intended to hide and wait for Grendel and then attack and kill the evil beast. A second band of warriors would wait inside the hall, just in case the monster succeeded in getting past the first group.

4   The Vikings hadn't been lying in wait for long when they spied a huge and fearsome creature approaching. They knew immediately that it was Grendel. Although the creature was stooped over, they could see that he was far taller than any ordinary man. As he came closer, they could see his green, horny skin. It was as tough as armor and could not be penetrated by even the sharpest sword. The men could also see Grendel's long, sharp teeth, which were curved like the tusks of a wild boar. The monster's hands ended in iron nails sharper than daggers. By Grendel's side hung an enormous bag, which he used to carry his victims back to the swamp where he could devour them one by one. But the most horrible of all

the demon's features was his hideous face. It was a swollen purple mass with eyes that regarded the world with pure hatred.

5   When the monster was almost upon them, the Vikings outside the hall fell upon him with their swords and spears. But Grendel's thick hide made their weapons useless. With a simple shrug of his powerful shoulders and a sweep of a huge arm, he threw off his attackers. Then he stormed to the door of the hall and blasted it open with a single blow. The Danes waiting inside were no more successful than their companions had been. None of their weapons made the slightest impact on the monster. As the men fought in vain, Grendel's iron claws slashed through their shields and armor. Soon many men had been killed or maimed. The remaining warriors could only watch in horror as the monster headed back toward his swamp, carrying several dead Vikings with him.

6   At about that time, tales of Grendel's gruesome deeds reached Sweden, where Prince Beowulf lived. Beowulf decided to go to the aid of King Hrothgar. He called together 14 of his bravest warriors and set sail with them for Denmark. When they reached King Hrothgar's kingdom, they received a warm welcome. The king escorted them to his drinking hall, where he lit a fire in the great fireplace and set

before them a feast of food and drink. During the feast, minstrels sang songs about the Viking heroes and their great deeds. Beowulf and his men enjoyed the drinking and boasting. Soon, however,

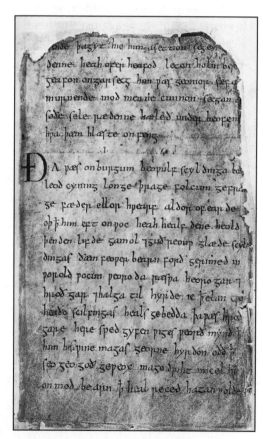

A page from an early version of Beowulf, *written in Old English about 1000* A.D.

Beowulf announced that it was time for the party to end. King Hrothgar and his people were asked to leave the hall, for Beowulf and his men had to prepare for their meeting with Grendel.

7   Beowulf's comrades lay down on the benches in the hall to await the arrival of the monster. They remained clothed in their heavy armor, in anticipation of a great struggle. Only Beowulf removed his shining coat of armor with its hundreds of interlocking steel rings. He unbuckled his sword and removed his helmet, saying to his men, "I will strive against this fiend weaponless. I will wrestle him with no armor, since he wears none. I will conquer, if I win, by my hand-grip alone."

8   Then Beowulf lay down next to his men. The fire in the fireplace provided the only light in the hall. Its flames cast strange shadows around the room. The men watched the shadows silently, waiting for the creature from the swamp. Suddenly there was a great crash. The massive wood and iron door shattered, and in burst the giant figure of Grendel. Before any of the warriors could move, Grendel's hand shot out toward one of Beowulf's men. The man screamed just once before his voice was cut off by a tearing sound. Almost instantly, Grendel had killed the man.

9   Then Grendel spotted Beowulf. The two sprang at each other in the same instant. Beowulf's hand reached out, caught one of the demon's hairy wrists, and hung fast. Grendel's iron claws reached for Beowulf's throat, but the prince moved more quickly than the monster. Giving the arm a fearful twist, Beowulf hurled Grendel to the floor. With one hand still holding firmly to the creature's wrist, Beowulf then leaped onto his back. The beast rolled and writhed on the floor in an effort to break free from the prince's grasp, but Beowulf hung on.

10   As the two struggled, they rolled closer and closer to the fireplace. Suddenly Grendel rolled right into the fire and hit his cheek against the burning coals. Shrieking in pain, he shook Beowulf from his shoulders. But even as the prince fell, he kept his grip on the monster's arm. At that point, Grendel wanted only to run back to his swamp. The burn on his face was agonizing, and he was in great pain from having his arm twisted around. He ran toward the doorway of the hall, dragging Beowulf with him.

11   As the monster struggled to get out the door, Beowulf placed one foot on either side of the door's inner frame. Then he gave Grendel's arm one last, mighty twist. There was a loud snap and an even louder bellow of pain. The monster's arm pulled out of its socket. Grendel fled screaming to his swamp, where he sank to the bottom and died. Back in the hall, Beowulf stood exhausted, still holding the monster's severed arm.

12   The next night, King Hrothgar held the most wonderful feast ever, in honor of Prince Beowulf. He gave Beowulf and his companions gifts of gold, jewels, horses, and armor, and he ordered his minstrels to write song-poems about Beowulf's heroic fight with Grendel.

13   The story of Beowulf and Grendel is itself part of a long heroic poem entitled *Beowulf*. Composed between the years 700 and 750, it is the oldest epic, or song-poem, in the English language. It is also the greatest piece of Old English literature. 🍃

If you have been timed while reading this article, enter your reading time below. Then turn to the Words-per-Minute Table on page 195 and look up your reading speed (words per minute). Enter your reading speed on the graph on page 196.

Reading Time: Lesson 15

_____ : _____
Minutes   Seconds

A | Finding the Main Idea

One statement below expresses the main idea of the article. One statement is too general, or too broad. The other statement explains only part of the article; it is too narrow. Label the statements using the following key:

M—Main Idea　　　**B—Too Broad**　　　**N—Too Narrow**

_____ 1. As told in an old poem, a Swedish prince helps the Danish Vikings defeat a terrible monster.

_____ 2. Beowulf killed the fearsome swamp monster Grendel by twisting his arm off.

_____ 3. In the epic poem _Beowulf_, the greatest piece of Old English literature, brave Prince Beowulf kills the evil swamp monster Grendel.

_____ Score 15 points for a correct M answer.

_____ Score 5 points for each correct B or N answer.

_____ **Total Score:** Finding the Main Idea

B | Recalling Facts

How well do you remember the facts in the article? Put an X in the box next to the answer that correctly completes each statement about the article.

1. The first thing King Hrothgar did to try to prevent Grendel from raiding his hall was
   - ☐ a. lay a trap for the monster.
   - ☐ b. strengthen the hall's doors with iron bands.
   - ☐ c. send for Beowulf.

2. Grendel's face was
   - ☐ a. green and scaly.
   - ☐ b. covered with slime.
   - ☐ c. purple and swollen.

3. Throughout the fight, Beowulf never let go of Grendel's
   - ☐ a. throat.
   - ☐ b. wrist.
   - ☐ c. hair.

4. Grendel was badly hurt by
   - ☐ a. burning coals from the fireplace.
   - ☐ b. the thrusting of the warriors' swords and spears.
   - ☐ c. Beowulf's dagger.

5. Beowulf wrenched out the monster's arm when he and Grendel
   - ☐ a. fell into the fireplace.
   - ☐ b. got to the swamp.
   - ☐ c. reached the doorway.

Score 5 points for each correct answer.

_____ **Total Score:** Recalling Facts

C Making Inferences

When you combine your own experience and information from a text to draw a conclusion that is not directly stated in that text, you are making an inference. Below are five statements that may or may not be inferences based on information in the article. Label the statements using the following key:

C—Correct Inference   **F—Faulty Inference**

_____ 1. The chief activity of the Vikings was the robbing and plundering of cities and ships.

_____ 2. Grendel was about 20 feet tall.

_____ 3. Grendel's chief food was the slime and other plants of the swamp.

_____ 4. Beowulf usually fought without wearing armor.

_____ 5. Beowulf believed in fighting fairly.

Score 5 points for each correct answer.

_____ **Total Score:** Making Inferences

D Using Words Precisely

Each numbered sentence below contains an underlined word or phrase from the article. Following the sentence are three definitions. One definition is closest to the meaning of the underlined word. One definition is opposite or nearly opposite. Label those two definitions using the following key. Do not label the remaining definition.

C—Closest   **O—Opposite or Nearly Opposite**

1. It was a swollen purple mass with eyes that <u>regarded</u> the world with pure hatred.

_____ a. threatened

_____ b. looked upon

_____ c. ignored

2. As the men fought <u>in vain</u>, Grendel's iron claws slashed through their shields and armor.

_____ a. successfully

_____ b. uselessly

_____ c. merrily

3. He said to his men, "I will <u>strive against</u> this fiend weaponless."

_____ a. struggle against

_____ b. speak with

_____ c. give in to

4. The king <u>escorted</u> them to his drinking hall, where he lit a fire in the great fireplace and set before them a feast of food and drink.

_____ a. accompanied

_____ b. sold

_____ c. abandoned

5. Back in the hall, Beowulf stood exhausted, still holding the monster's <u>severed</u> arm.

_____ a. disgusting

_____ b. attached

_____ c. torn off

_____ Score 3 points for each correct C answer.

_____ Score 2 points for each correct O answer.

_____ **Total Score:** Using Words Precisely

Enter the four total scores in the spaces below, and add them together to find your Reading Comprehension Score. Then record your score on the graph on page 197.

Score	Question Type	Lesson 15
_____	Finding the Main Idea	
_____	Recalling Facts	
_____	Making Inferences	
_____	Using Words Precisely	
_____	**Reading Comprehension Score**	

Author's Approach

Put an X in the box next to the correct answer.

1. The main purpose of the first paragraph is to

☐ a. express a negative opinion about the lifestyle of King Hrothgar and his Vikings.

☐ b. inform the reader about King Hrothgar's drinking hall.

☐ c. explain why King Hrothgar and his Vikings should have been happy.

2. From the statements below, choose those that you believe the author would agree with.

☐ a. Any one of Beowulf's brave warriors could have defeated Grendel.

☐ b. King Hrothgar owed Beowulf a great debt of gratitude.

☐ c. Grendel was surprised and alarmed by Beowulf's attack.

3. From Beowulf's statement "'I will wrestle him with no armor, since he wears none'," you can conclude that the author wants the reader to think that the prince

☐ a. was strong, brave, and fair.

☐ b. dreaded his battle with Grendel.

☐ c. underestimated Grendel's strength.

4. The author probably wrote this article in order to

☐ a. describe Grendel's murderous raids.

☐ b. describe what life was like in Denmark centuries ago.

☐ c. tell the reader the story of Beowulf and Grendel.

_____ Number of correct answers

Record your personal assessment of your work on the Critical Thinking Chart on page 198.

Summarizing and Paraphrasing

Follow the directions provided for question 1. Put an X in the box next to the correct answer for question 2.

1. Complete the following one-sentence summary of the article using the lettered phrases from the phrase bank below. Write the letters on the lines.

> **Phrase Bank:**
> a. Beowulf's decision to help the king
> b. a description of Grendel's murderous attacks on King Hrothgar's Vikings
> c. Grendel's death at the hands of Beowulf

After a brief description of the Viking way of life, the article about Grendel begins with _____, goes on to explain _____, and ends with _____.

2. Choose the best one-sentence paraphrase for the following sentence from the article:

"When the monster was almost upon them, the Vikings outside the hall fell upon him with their swords and spears."

☐ a. When Grendel drew near, the Vikings attacked him with their weapons.

☐ b. The Vikings stumbled and fell on their swords just before Grendel arrived.

☐ c. When Grendel approached, the Vikings tripped over their weapons and fell on him.

> _____ Number of correct answers
>
> Record your personal assessment of your work on the Critical Thinking Chart on page 198.

Critical Thinking

Put an X in the box next to the correct answer for questions 1, 4, and 5. Follow the directions provided for the other questions.

1. From the article, you can predict that if Beowulf hadn't aided King Hrothgar,

☐ a. someone else would have succeeded in killing Grendel.

☐ b. Grendel would have continued to kill the king's warriors.

☐ c. Grendel would have grown tired of killing the king's warriors.

2. Choose from the letters below to correctly complete the following statement. Write the letters on the lines.

On the positive side, _____, but on the negative side _____.

a. Hrothgar's celebrations usually ended with everyone falling asleep

b. Hrothgar and his men lived in splendor in Denmark

c. a horrifying creature had terrorized the kingdom for 12 years

3. Choose from the letters below to correctly complete the following statement. Write the letters on the lines.

According to the article, news of Grendel's gruesome deeds caused _____ to _____, and the effect was _____.

a. offer to help Hrothgar

b. Beowulf killed Grendel with his bare hands

c. Beowulf

4. How is Grendel an example of a monster?

☐ a. Grendel ran away even after his arm had been pulled out of its socket.

☐ b. Grendel was a hideous, evil creature who lived in a swamp.

☐ c. Grendel's battle with Beowulf is part of the oldest epic in the English language.

5. What did you have to do to answer question 1?

☐ a. find a cause (why something happened)

☐ b. find a reason (why something is the way it is)

☐ c. make a prediction (what might happen next)

_____ Number of correct answers

Record your personal assessment of your work on the Critical Thinking Chart on page 198.

Personal Response

A question I would like answered by Beowulf is

_____

_____

_____

_____

Self-Assessment

I'm proud of how I answered question # _____ in section _____ because

_____

_____

_____

_____

CRITICAL THINKING

CHUPACABRA
Bloodthirsty Beast

The panic began in 1995 in Puerto Rico. Farmers began finding the bloodless corpses of goats, chickens, rabbits, dogs, sheep, pigs, and other animals. The victims had all had their blood drained through puncture wounds, usually in the neck or chest. The killings soon reached epidemic proportions in the hills of Puerto Rico. Was this the work of wild animals? Or was it the work of some supernatural beast with a vampire's thirst for blood?

2 To many people, the answer was obvious—the grim massacre was the handiwork of a strange monster described as part bat, part kangaroo, and part insect, with a little bit of reptile and armadillo tossed in for good measure. People who have seen the creature report that it is only three to four feet tall. Still, it is one scary sight. It has fangs, a row of spikes running down its back, and bulging red eyes that look like burning coal. It also has bat wings and kangaroo legs. In Puerto Rico and other Spanish-speaking places, the beast has been given a name that reminds everyone of its love for

This illustration of the Chupacabra, or goatsucker, is based on eyewitness descriptions.

goat's blood. It is called *Chupacabra*, which is Spanish for "goat sucker."

3   Whoever or whatever the Chupacabra is, it must have some relatives. After all, it seems to have been in more than one place at a time. Chupacabras have been sighted in San Francisco, Miami, San Antonio, New York City, and even London and Moscow. They have also been spotted in Costa Rica, Peru, and Ecuador. But the gruesome little creatures have done their worst mischief in Puerto Rico and Mexico.

4   In Mexico, the monster has caused genuine fear and panic. In 1996, the *Los Angeles Times* ran a story about the creature. The headline read: "Tales of Bloodthirsty Beast Terrify Mexico." A *Reuters* headline put it this way: "Mysterious Vampire Beast Spreads Panic in Mexico." The *Tucson Weekly* did a cover story on Chupacabras. It was titled "Hellmonkeys from Beyond."

5   Where do the Chupacabras come from? Some people say they must have come down to Earth from outer space. Others think they are mutants—the results of an experiment gone wrong. People swear that wherever this demon came from, it is not a creature one might find in the wild or in a zoo.

6   And so while skeptics laughed off the Chupacabra, many other people are nearly scared to death. Take the case of Naucalpan, a small village in the Mexican state of Sinaloa. There a local farmer saw a batlike creature swoop down on his corral and kill 24 of his sheep. All the dead animals had puncture marks on their necks, and their blood had been sucked until their bodies were as dry as bone.

7   A major Mexican TV network rushed a camera crew to Naucalpan. It broadcast news of the attack across Mexico. "This created a great panic," said Desiderio Aquilar, a Sinaloa police official. Many people felt certain that Chupacabra was to

A Mexican farmer herds goats in the area where the Chupacabra is said to have struck.

blame for the deaths. "Mothers have quit sending their children to schools for fear they could be attacked on the way," said Aquilar. "Farmers who used to start work at 4 A.M. to beat the heat aren't leaving their homes until well after daybreak." In some places, farmers armed with torches attacked bats in their caves, hoping to burn out any Chupacabras who might be hiding there.

8   More reports of attacks and killings flooded in from other parts of Mexico. In the town of Villalba, 20 roosting chickens were found dead. All had holes in their chests. Victor Santiago, the chief of police, was stunned. He said, "We have no explanation because it is difficult [for any killer] to catch a chicken that's asleep in a tree. It's a very strange case. A very complicated case."

9   In a few instances, a Chupacabra is reported to have attacked humans. A 21-year-old woman claimed that one of these beasts bit off her ear. In another widely reported case, a Chupacabra supposedly hopped through a young boy's open bedroom window and landed on him, smelling "like a wet dog." Although the boy wasn't hurt, his aunt was called in to give her opinion of the event. Without hesitation she said that the footprints on the little boy's chest were made by a Chupacabra. Angel Pulido, a Mexican farmer, called in reporters to show them bite marks on his right arm, which he claimed he got from "a giant bat that looked like a witch."

10   There was also a Chupacabra panic in Puerto Rico. In the small town of Canovanas, 30 people reported seeing a weird creature swoop out of the sky and leap over trees. Meanwhile, animals kept turning up dead with puncture wounds in their necks and chests. Ismael Aguayo was a police detective who checked out the reports. He said, "We are all very worried here. Our animals are dying at an alarming rate…. But we are worried that our children will be next."

11   Not everyone in Mexico or Puerto Rico thinks that the ghoulish killings were done by Chupacabras. Most investigators blamed the attacks on wild dogs or cougars. In Mexico, to calm fears, federal experts conducted autopsies in Sinaloa on dead sheep. They concluded that the attacks had been made by coyotes or other natural predators.

12   These experts also set traps to prove that wild predators, not the supernatural Chupacabra, were killing the animals. They put live sheep in the same corral where the first killings had taken place. All-night guards watched the corral. "Late at night, a few wild dogs showed up and attacked the sheep—leaving the same marks found on the first dead sheep," said Desiderio Aquilar. The investigators then captured the dogs and showed them to the townspeople.

13   Still, even this evidence cannot stop the public's fear of Chupacabras. Too many people have seen too much with their own eyes to be convinced that the Chupacabras are not a danger. Hector Armstrong, a Princeton University student who started his own web page on Chupacabras, thinks outsiders shouldn't dismiss those eyewitness accounts. "While it's funny to laugh about the Chupacabras," he said, "we should not discount the mounds of evidence people have found, nor should we disrespect the reports of hundreds of people."

If you have been timed while reading this article, enter your reading time below. Then turn to the Words-per-Minute Table on page 195 and look up your reading speed (words per minute). Enter your reading speed on the graph on page 196.

Reading Time: **Lesson 16**

_____ : _____

Minutes   Seconds

A | Finding the Main Idea

One statement below expresses the main idea of the article. One statement is too general, or too broad. The other statement explains only part of the article; it is too narrow. Label the statements using the following key:

M—Main Idea   **B—Too Broad**   **N—Too Narrow**

_____ 1. A farmer in Naucalpan saw a strange creature swoop down on his corral and kill 24 of his sheep.

_____ 2. People who claim to have seen Chupacabra say that it is not a normal creature.

_____ 3. In countries such as Puerto Rico and Mexico, people have reported seeing a strange batlike creature that drains the blood from its animal victims.

_____ Score 15 points for a correct M answer.

_____ Score 5 points for each correct B or N answer.

_____ **Total Score:** Finding the Main Idea

B | Recalling Facts

How well do you remember the facts in the article? Put an X in the box next to the answer that correctly completes each statement about the article.

1. *Chupacabra* is Spanish for
   - ☐ a. "goat sucker."
   - ☐ b. "blood sucker."
   - ☐ c. "hell monkey."

2. Some eyewitnesses think that Chupacabras came from
   - ☐ a. London.
   - ☐ b. a zoo.
   - ☐ c. outer space.

3. All of the dead animals in Naucalpan
   - ☐ a. had footprints on their chests.
   - ☐ b. had had their ears bitten off.
   - ☐ c. had puncture marks on their necks.

4. After a Chupacabra attack in Canovanas, many people feared that
   - ☐ a. Ismael Aguayo might be attacked next.
   - ☐ b. their children might be attacked next.
   - ☐ c. others might not believe their stories.

5. When investigators set a trap by placing live sheep in a corral,
   - ☐ a. Chupacabra showed up and attacked the sheep.
   - ☐ b. a few wild dogs attacked the sheep.
   - ☐ c. a few bats attacked the sheep.

_____ Score 5 points for each correct answer.

_____ **Total Score:** Recalling Facts

C | Making Inferences

When you combine your own experience and information from a text to draw a conclusion that is not directly stated in that text, you are making an inference. Below are five statements that may or may not be inferences based on information in the article. Label the statements using the following key:

C—Correct Inference   **F—Faulty Inference**

_____ 1. Chupacabras are compared to vampires because vampires are supposed to suck the blood out of their victims.

_____ 2. Chupacabras have been blamed for killing many goats.

_____ 3. Desiderio Aquilar believes that the Chupacabra attack in Naucalpan was actually carried out by wild dogs.

_____ 4. No one believes that Chupacabras would attack humans.

_____ 5. If evidence revealed that coyotes or other natural predators were responsible for some animal attacks, everyone would stop believing in Chupacabras.

Score 5 points for each correct answer.

_____ **Total Score:** Making Inferences

D | Using Words Precisely

Each numbered sentence below contains an underlined word or phrase from the article. Following the sentence are three definitions. One definition is closest to the meaning of the underlined word. One definition is opposite or nearly opposite. Label those two definitions using the following key. Do not label the remaining definition.

C—Closest   **O—Opposite or Nearly Opposite**

1. The killings soon reached <u>epidemic</u> proportions in the hills of Puerto Rico.

_____ a. restricted

_____ b. widespread

_____ c. sad

2. Others thought they were <u>mutants</u>—the results of an experiment gone wrong.

_____ a. normal creatures

_____ b. aliens from outer space

_____ c. creatures that have been drastically changed

3. People swore that wherever this <u>demon</u> came from, it was not a creature one might find in the wild or in a zoo.

_____ a. animal

_____ b. angel

_____ c. evil spirit

4. Victor Santiago, the chief of police, was <u>stunned</u>.

_____ a. not surprised

_____ b. shocked

_____ c. killed

5. Not everyone in Mexico or Puerto Rico thought that the <u>ghoulish</u> killings were done by Chupacabras.

_____ a. wholesome

_____ b. local

_____ c. creepy

_____ Score 3 points for each correct C answer.

_____ Score 2 points for each correct O answer.

_____ **Total Score:** Using Words Precisely

Enter the four total scores in the spaces below, and add them together to find your Reading Comprehension Score. Then record your score on the graph on page 197.

Score	Question Type	Lesson 16
_____	Finding the Main Idea	
_____	Recalling Facts	
_____	Making Inferences	
_____	Using Words Precisely	
_____	**Reading Comprehension Score**	

Author's Approach

Put an X in the box next to the correct answer.

1. The author uses the first sentence of the article to

☐ a. inform the reader that something caused a panic in Puerto Rico in 1995.

☐ b. describe Puerto Rico.

☐ c. persuade the reader to visit Puerto Rico.

2. What does the author mean by the statement "People swear that wherever this demon came from, it is not a creature one might find in the wild or in a zoo"?

☐ a. Most people thought that the Chupacabra was too wild to live in a zoo.

☐ b. Most people wanted to put the Chupacabra in the zoo.

☐ c. Chupacabra didn't look like an animal anyone had ever seen before.

3. Choose the statement below that best explains how the author addresses the opposing point of view in the article.

☐ a. To those who claim that Chupacabras don't exist, the author points to the eyewitness accounts of hundreds of people.

☐ b. To those who claim that Chupacabras don't exist, the author cites the findings of federal experts who conducted autopsies on dead sheep in Sinaloa.

☐ c. To those who claim that Chupacabras don't exist, the author describes the experience of investigators who set a trap for the creature.

4. The author probably wrote this article in order to

- [ ] a. express an opinion about Chupacabras.
- [ ] b. inform the reader about Chupacabras.
- [ ] c. convince the reader that Chupacabras do not exist.

_____ Number of correct answers

Record your personal assessment of your work on the Critical Thinking Chart on page 198.

Summarizing and Paraphrasing

Put an X in the box next to the correct answer.

1. Below are summaries of the article. Choose the summary that says all the most important things about the article but in the fewest words.

- [ ] a. Chupacabras have attacked and killed many animals. The creatures make puncture wounds in their victims' neck or chest and drain all the blood.

- [ ] b. Chupacabras have reportedly attacked and drained the blood from many animals in Puerto Rico and Mexico. Although evidence has suggested that Chupacabras are actually wild dogs or other natural predators, many people remain unconvinced.

- [ ] c. Bloodthirsty Chupacabra attacks have been reported in many parts of the world, but most have occurred in Puerto Rico and Mexico. Chupacabras, which eyewitnesses have described as part bat and part kangaroo, reportedly drain the blood from their animal victims. There have also been a few instances of Chupacabra attacks on humans.

2. Choose the sentence that correctly restates the following sentence from the article:

"In another widely reported case, a Chupacabra supposedly hopped through a young boy's open bedroom window and landed on him, smelling 'like a wet dog.'"

- [ ] a. In one well-known case, Chupacabra jumped on a boy who smelled like a wet dog.

- [ ] b. In one well-known case, a boy thought that Chupacabra jumped into his room, but it turned out to be a wet dog.

- [ ] c. In one well-known case, the Chupacabra that jumped into a boy's bedroom smelled like a wet dog.

_____ Number of correct answers

Record your personal assessment of your work on the Critical Thinking Chart on page 198.

Critical Thinking

Put an X in the box next to the correct answer for questions 1, 2, and 4. Follow the directions provided for question 3.

1. Which of the following statements from the article is an opinion rather than a fact?

- [ ] a. "The *Tucson Weekly* did a cover story on Chupacabras."

- [ ] b. "In Mexico, to calm fears, federal experts conducted autopsies in Sinaloa on dead sheep."

- [ ] c. "'While it's funny to laugh about the Chupacabras,…we should not discount the mounds of evidence people have found, nor should we disrespect the reports of hundreds of people.'"

2. From what Victor Santiago said in paragraph 8, you can predict that he believes that

☐ a. natural predators killed the chickens in Villalba.

☐ b. a Chupacabra may have been responsible for the dead chickens in Villalba.

☐ c. the chickens in Villalba may have been shot.

3. Choose from the letters below to correctly complete the following statement. Write the letters on the lines.

According to the article, the attack in Sinaloa caused _____ to _____, and the effect was _____.

a. mothers were afraid to send their children to school

b. broadcast news of the attack across Mexico

c. a major Mexican TV network

4. If you were an investigator, how could you use the information in the article to lessen residents' fears following a reported Chupacabra attack?

☐ a. Conduct a controlled experiment like the one in which sheep were used as bait for predators and inform residents of your findings.

☐ b. Have a TV network broadcast news of the attack.

☐ c. Admit that you are baffled by the complicated case.

_____ Number of correct answers

Record your personal assessment of your work on the Critical Thinking Chart on page 198.

Personal Response

I can't believe

_____

_____

_____

_____

Self-Assessment

One of the things I did best when reading this article was

_____

_____

_____

_____

I believe I did this well because

_____

_____

_____

_____

CRITICAL THINKING

DRACULA
Terror in Transylvania

Dracula, also known as Vlad the Impaler, dines amid bodies he has had impaled in this 15th-century German woodcut.

They come in the night, flying from their graves in the form of bats. If they are not stopped, they will kill the members of their own families, and then go on to take the lives of others. They are vampires—corpses that rise from their coffins in the middle of the night, seeking out living victims whose blood they drink to sustain their unnatural existence.

2 The most famous of all vampires is Count Dracula, a fictional character made famous in books and movies. Dracula is portrayed as a tall, dark figure with two long fangs. He wears a black cape lined with red silk. As is true of all vampires, he can abandon his coffin only after the sun has set, and he must return to it before sunrise, for he cannot survive in the light of day. He attacks his victims by piercing their necks with his fangs and sucking out their blood. A vampire's victims also become vampires (although according to some stories, it takes three bites to bring that about).

3 Like Count Dracula, a newly created vampire will live forever, roaming the

lands in the dark of night to find its own victims. There is only one way the monster can be stopped: someone must drive a wooden stake through its heart.

4 Although the legend of Dracula the vampire is not true, there was once a real Count Dracula. Like the vampire of fiction and film, he lived in the mountainous part of eastern Europe known as Transylvania. He was born to nobility in 1431, and while his real name was Vlad, he was called by his nickname, Dracula, which means "son of the dragon." He was also known as Vlad the Impaler, a nickname he earned for the barbaric acts he committed.

5 In the 15th century, Turkish warriors were conquering much of southeastern Europe. When Dracula was 13, the Turks captured his father. In order to secure his own freedom, the father gave Dracula to the Turks as a hostage. For the next four years, Dracula was imprisoned in a Turkish jail.

6 Perhaps it was his father's betrayal that warped Dracula's mind, but whatever the reason, from 1448 on, Dracula was renowned as a fierce and evil madman. After his imprisonment, he returned to rule his native Transylvania. His main job was to defend it against the Turks, and he himself led many battles against the

invaders. But he also murdered thousands of his own countrymen. There was usually no reason for the killings except that they gave Dracula pleasure.

7 His favorite method of killing was impalement. Many times he ordered his servants to prepare hundreds of long wooden stakes. He wanted the tips of the stakes to be rounded a bit—not so sharp that his victims would die quickly. Then the torture would begin. Dracula would order the stakes to be driven through the entire lengths of his victims' bodies. The stakes would later be erected on the hills around the town, and the maimed people would be left there to suffer a slow and agonizing death.

8 For several years, Dracula terrorized the people of Transylvania with such monstrous deeds. Perhaps his single greatest crime occurred on the morning of August 24, 1460. On that day, Dracula ordered thirty thousand Transylvanians impaled on stakes around the city of Brasov.

9 Dracula's crazed acts also had a powerful effect on the invading Turks. As an army of Turks approached one Transylvanian town in 1460, they were horrified by what they saw. There outside the city were the remains of twenty thousand men rotting on wooden stakes.

The men, most of whom were members of the upper class, had been Dracula's prisoners. All had offended Dracula in some way. Repulsed by the sight, the Turks turned away.

Gary Oldman and Winona Ryder star in the 1992 film Bram Stoker's Dracula.

10   At last the Turks did succeed in invading Transylvania and capturing Dracula. Although his rule was ended, word of his gruesome deeds lived on and soon became legend.

11   One other historical figure whose habits became part of the vampire legend was Countess Elizabeth Bathory. Also from Transylvania, she lived during the 17th century. One day a maid who was combing Elizabeth's hair pulled one strand a little too hard. Angered, the countess slapped the girl so forcefully that blood appeared on the girl's cheek. A few drops of the blood splattered onto the countess's hand, and to Elizabeth's twisted mind, the blood seemed to have the effect of making her skin as firm and fresh as that of the young maid. The countess quickly summoned her servants and ordered the girl killed so that her blood could be drained into a tub. Elizabeth bathed in the blood and believed that it made her look younger.

12   Over the next 10 years, the countess had many young maidens killed in order to bathe in their blood. Finally one day a girl escaped and ran to notify the king. It was only then that the countess was arrested and her grisly ritual halted.

13   Stories about such characters as Elizabeth Bathory and Vlad the Impaler were passed down through the years, eventually becoming part of the general folklore of eastern Europe. The legend of Dracula was brought to the West by Bram Stoker, who in the late 1800s wrote the first novel about the vampire.

14   Since then, interest in Dracula has grown in both western Europe and America. Over a hundred vampire films have been made. Bela Lugosi was the first American movie Dracula, and he remains the most famous. Lugosi so loved the role that in his will he requested that he be buried in his Dracula costume, cape and all. 🍃

If you have been timed while reading this article, enter your reading time below. Then turn to the Words-per-Minute Table on page 195 and look up your reading speed (words per minute). Enter your reading speed on the graph on page 196.

Reading Time: Lesson 17

_____ : _____

Minutes   Seconds

A | Finding the Main Idea

One statement below expresses the main idea of the article. One statement is too general, or too broad. The other statement explains only part of the article; it is too narrow. Label the statements using the following key:

M—Main Idea   **B—Too Broad**   **N—Too Narrow**

_____ 1. The fictional character Count Dracula was created by combining the insane traits of some real people.

_____ 2. The fictional vampire Count Dracula is based on a real Transylvanian Dracula and a mad Transylvanian countess.

_____ 3. In Transylvania in the 15th century, there was a real Count Dracula, whose nickname was Vlad the Impaler.

_____ Score 15 points for a correct M answer.

_____ Score 5 points for each correct B or N answer.

_____ **Total Score:** Finding the Main Idea

B | Recalling Facts

How well do you remember the facts in the article? Put an X in the box next to the answer that correctly completes each statement about the article.

1. Vlad the Impaler was
   - ☐ a. the ruler of Transylvania.
   - ☐ b. a barbaric Turk.
   - ☐ c. the father of Countess Elizabeth Bathory.

2. Vlad got rid of Turkish invaders by
   - ☐ a. offering them hostages.
   - ☐ b. impaling them.
   - ☐ c. erecting impaled victims for them to see.

3. The most famous Dracula of the movies was
   - ☐ a. Lon Chaney.
   - ☐ b. Bela Lugosi.
   - ☐ c. Vincent Price.

4. Countess Elizabeth Bathory
   - ☐ a. bathed in blood.
   - ☐ b. drank blood.
   - ☐ c. pierced the necks of her young maids.

5. Countess Elizabeth Bathory lived in
   - ☐ a. England.
   - ☐ b. Transylvania.
   - ☐ c. France.

Score 5 points for each correct answer.

_____ **Total Score:** Recalling Facts

C Making Inferences

When you combine your own experience and information from a text to draw a conclusion that is not directly stated in that text, you are making an inference. Below are five statements that may or may not be inferences based on information in the article. Label the statements using the following key:

C—Correct Inference   **F—Faulty Inference**

_____ 1. The Turks who finally conquered Transylvania were kind rulers.

_____ 2. The people of Transylvania felt that they were powerless to stop Count Dracula.

_____ 3. Vlad became insane because of the torture he underwent during his four years in a Turkish jail.

_____ 4. Some of Countess Elizabeth Bathory's servants helped her continue her ghastly ritual of bathing in blood.

_____ 5. Bram Stoker, who wrote the first novel about Count Dracula, believed in the existence of vampires.

Score 5 points for each correct answer.

_____ **Total Score:** Making Inferences

D Using Words Precisely

Each numbered sentence below contains an underlined word or phrase from the article. Following the sentence are three definitions. One definition is closest to the meaning of the underlined word. One definition is opposite or nearly opposite. Label those two definitions using the following key. Do not label the remaining definition.

C—Closest   **O—Opposite or Nearly Opposite**

1. They are vampires—corpses that rise from their coffins in the middle of the night, seeking out living victims whose blood they drink to <u>sustain</u> their unnatural existence.

    _____ a. confuse

    _____ b. support

    _____ c. end

2. In order to <u>secure</u> his own freedom, the father gave Dracula to the Turks as a hostage.

    _____ a. gain

    _____ b. question

    _____ c. lose

3. <u>Repulsed</u> by the sight, the Turks turned away.

    _____ a. influenced

    _____ b. disgusted

    _____ c. attracted

4. Perhaps it was his father's betrayal that warped Dracula's mind, but whatever the reason, from 1448 on, Dracula was <u>renowned</u> as a fierce and evil madman.

_____ a. unknown

_____ b. replaced

_____ c. widely recognized

5. It was only then that the countess was arrested and her <u>grisly</u> ritual halted.

_____ a. ghastly

_____ b. daily

_____ c. appealing

_____ Score 3 points for each correct C answer.

_____ Score 2 points for each correct O answer.

_____ **Total Score:** Using Words Precisely

Enter the four total scores in the spaces below, and add them together to find your Reading Comprehension Score. Then record your score on the graph on page 197.

Score	Question Type	Lesson 17
_____	Finding the Main Idea	
_____	Recalling Facts	
_____	Making Inferences	
_____	Using Words Precisely	
_____	**Reading Comprehension Score**	

Author's Approach

Put an X in the box next to the correct answer.

1. What is the author's purpose in writing "Dracula: Terror in Transylvania"?

☐ a. To inform the reader about some of the true stories that helped create the Dracula legend

☐ b. To inform the reader about the monster in vampire movies

☐ c. To compare the fictional Dracula to Vlad the Impaler

2. Which of the following statements from the article best describes the real Count Dracula?

☐ a. "He [Dracula] wears a black cape lined with red silk."

☐ b. "He attacks his victims by piercing their necks with his fangs and sucking out their blood."

☐ c. "Perhaps it was his father's betrayal that warped Dracula's mind, but whatever the reason, from 1448 on, Dracula was renowned as a fierce and evil madman."

3. From the statements below, choose those that you believe the author would agree with.

☐ a. The fictional Dracula's fondness for drinking blood springs, in part, from the bloody deeds of Vlad the Impaler and Elizabeth Bathory.

☐ b. The role of Dracula was Bela Lugosi's favorite.

☐ c. Vlad and Elizabeth felt very guilty for what they did.

CRITICAL THINKING

4. The author tells this story mainly by

☐ a. telling the story of Vlad the Impaler.

☐ b. comparing Vlad the Impaler to Elizabeth Bathory.

☐ c. retelling some of the stories that have created the Dracula legend.

_____ Number of correct answers

Record your personal assessment of your work on the Critical Thinking Chart on page 198.

Summarizing and Paraphrasing

Put an X in the box next to the correct answer.

1. Below are summaries of the article. Choose the summary that says all the most important things about the article but in the fewest words.

☐ a. The fictional Count Dracula is based partly on the bloody deeds of Vlad the Impaler and Elizabeth Bathory, who both lived in Transylvania. The character of Dracula was introduced to the West by Bram Stoker, who wrote the first novel about the vampire. Since then, interest in Dracula has grown, and more than a hundred vampire films have been made.

☐ b. Although over one hundred films about Dracula have been made, the first one starring Bela Lugosi remains the most famous.

☐ c. Dracula is based partly on the bloody deeds of two Transylvanian nobles. After the first novel about Dracula appeared, interest in the character grew. Many movies have since been made about vampires.

2. Read the statement about the article below. Then read the paraphrase of that statement. Choose the reason that best tells why the paraphrase does not say the same thing as the statement.

Statement: Vlad killed his victims by driving a long wooden stake through the lengths of their bodies and then leaving the maimed people to die a slow, agonizing death.

Paraphrase: To kill people, Vlad ordered long wooden stakes—with slightly rounded tips—driven through the lengths of his victim's bodies, and then he had the stakes erected on the hills around the town where the tortured people would remain until they died.

☐ a. Paraphrase says too much.

☐ b. Paraphrase doesn't say enough.

☐ c. Paraphrase doesn't agree with the statement about the article.

_____ Number of correct answers

Record your personal assessment of your work on the Critical Thinking Chart on page 198.

Critical Thinking

Follow the directions provided for question 1, 3, and 5. Put an X in the box next to the correct answer for the other questions.

1. For each statement below, write O if it expresses an opinion and write F if it expresses a fact.

_____ a. Vlad the Impaler was a real person.

_____ b. Bela Lugosi was buried in his Dracula costume.

_____ c. Little children should not be told the story of Dracula because it is too frightening.

2. Judging from Vlad's actions as told in this article, you can conclude that

☐ a. he was actually a vampire.

☐ b. he was well loved.

☐ c. the people of Transylvania hated and feared him.

3. Using what you know about the fictional Dracula and what is told about Vlad the Impaler in the article, name three ways Dracula is similar to Vlad and three ways he is different from Vlad. Cite the paragraph number(s) where you found details in the article to support your conclusions.

Similarities

_____

_____

_____

Differences

_____

_____

_____

4. What was the cause of Elizabeth Bathory's arrest?

☐ a. Elizabeth slapped one of her maids very hard.

☐ b. A young girl escaped and told the king about Elizabeth's murderous deeds.

☐ c. Elizabeth's grisly ritual was stopped.

5. In which paragraph did you find the information or details to answer question 4?

_____

_____ Number of correct answers

Record your personal assessment of your work on the Critical Thinking Chart on page 198.

Personal Response

What was most surprising or interesting to you about this article?

_____

_____

_____

_____

Self-Assessment

Before reading this article, I already knew

_____

_____

_____

_____

CRITICAL THINKING

ZOMBIES
The Walking Dead

In Haiti some years ago, a group of girls on a shopping trip stepped into a store. As they looked around, a salesgirl walked over to wait on them. When the girls saw the salesgirl, they recognized her as an old friend. But instead of being happy to meet someone they knew, the girls were terrified. The salesgirl had been dead for three years!

2   Most people in that situation might have assumed that the salesgirl simply bore a close resemblance to their dead friend. But the girls were Haitian and, like a good number of people in Haiti, they believed in another explanation. They believed that the salesgirl was a zombie.

3   A zombie is someone who is supposedly not alive but not exactly dead either. Zombies are believed to be people who have died and been buried, but who have later been raised from their graves and turned into slaves. For that reason, they are sometimes referred to as the "walking dead." Their gaze is usually a blank stare, and their movements are slow and mechanical. They can work, but only at simple jobs that don't call for any thought. They do only what they are told to do.

A Haitian voodoo priest sits at an altar surrounded by the tools of his trade.

4   Belief in zombies is tied to a belief in voodoo, a religion that developed in Africa. When Africans were brought to the New World as slaves, they brought voodoo with them. Many of those African slaves were taken to the Caribbean island of Haiti, and even today, long after the end of slavery in Haiti, voodoo is practiced on the island. Although voodoo has spread to parts of both North and South America, Haiti remains the center for voodoo.

5   The most powerful person in the world of voodoo is the *houngan*, or voodoo priest. Houngans are said to have many powers. Among them is the power to raise the dead. It is the houngan who commands corpses to rise from their graves, and it is he who turns the corpses into zombies. Once a zombie has been created, the houngan has absolute control over him or her. Zombies have no minds of their own; they will do only what the houngan commands them. If he tells them to walk, they will walk. If he orders them to pick sugar cane, that is what they will do. Frequently a houngan uses his zombies to do farm work for him, and occasionally he rents them out to other farmers.

6   Most of the stories about zombies come from poor, uneducated people. Skeptics point out that in Haiti people in those circumstances tend to be very superstitious, and therefore, they are not the most reliable sources. But a well-educated man told the following story of meeting a zombie. The man was driving in the country when his car broke down in front of a house he had never noticed

Voodoo practices are still present in modern-day Haiti. Here people perform a voodoo ceremony in a street of the capital, Port-au-Prince.

before. The owner of the house, a houngan, invited the man inside. The houngan explained that he had caused the car to break down because he wanted the man to meet somebody. The houngan then brought out a zombie. The startled man recognized the zombie as a friend he hadn't seen in a year.

7   Another Haitian zombie was seen by many people and was even photographed. Her story is famous. She showed up one day on a farm where people recognized her. The people remembered her as a relative of the owner of the farm. They also remembered that she had died several years earlier. Everyone who had known the woman was sure that it was the same person. The people accused the dead woman's husband of poisoning his wife and then paying a houngan to turn her into a zombie. The mystery has never been cleared up, and some people continue to believe that voodoo is responsible for this bizarre occurrence. Others, however, have suggested other explanations.

8   One possibility is that the dead woman's relatives had hired an impostor to pose as the zombie. If they hated the dead woman's husband and wanted to get him in trouble, that was one way to do it. Accusing him of conspiring with a houngan was a sure way of making trouble for him.

9   Another explanation is that the woman had never died, but had been drugged by the houngan. In a heavily drugged state, she had been believed dead. A few hours after she was buried, the houngan dug her up again and made her his slave. He kept her drugged from then on, in order to keep her in his power. Many people who have studied voodoo believe that this is how zombies are made. The houngans have great power in the eyes of those who believe in voodoo. His followers do not question his ability to raise the dead. They both fear and respect him.

10   Some zombies have been proved to be fakes. One investigator, for instance, tells of accompanying a houngan and his assistant to a graveyard to watch them create a zombie. First the assistant dug up a coffin and opened it. The houngan uttered some magic words over the body and poured a liquid on it. Then the corpse sat up, got out of the coffin and, moving as though in a trance, walked away with the houngan. The whole thing looked real, but the investigator was suspicious.

11   The next day, the investigator went back to the cemetery for another look at the empty grave. As he looked around, he discovered an air hose leading down to where the coffin had been. When he saw that, he realized that the creation of the zombie had been a trick. The "zombie" had never been dead. Rather, a living person had been lying in the coffin, breathing through the air hose and waiting to be dug up.

12   Most Haitians don't believe in zombies, but those who do have influenced the country's burial customs. It is said that the families of some dead people take turns guarding the graves of their loved ones. They stand guard for several weeks after the person has been buried. Only then do they feel it is safe to end their vigil. They figure that by then the corpse is too decomposed to be of use to any houngan who might want to turn it into a slave.

13   Is there really such a thing as voodoo magic? Voodoo exists as long as people believe in it. By believing in the houngans, the people give them power, just as a magician works real magic in the eyes of trusting and innocent children.

If you have been timed while reading this article, enter your reading time below. Then turn to the Words-per-Minute Table on page 195 and look up your reading speed (words per minute). Enter your reading speed on the graph on page 196.

Reading Time: **Lesson 18**

_____ : _____
Minutes   Seconds

Finding the Main Idea

One statement below expresses the main idea of the article. One statement is too general, or too broad. The other statement explains only part of the article; it is too narrow. Label the statements using the following key:

M—Main Idea   B—Too Broad   N—Too Narrow

_____ 1. People who believe in voodoo believe that voodoo priests can create zombies—raise dead people and have power over them.

_____ 2. Some people believe that zombies are actually people who have been heavily drugged by voodoo priests.

_____ 3. Zombies, or the "walking dead," are part of the religion called voodoo.

_____ Score 15 points for a correct M answer.

_____ Score 5 points for each correct B or N answer.

_____ **Total Score:** Finding the Main Idea

B **Recalling Facts**

How well do you remember the facts in the article? Put an X in the box next to the answer that correctly completes each statement about the article.

1. Houngans frequently use zombies
   ☐ a. to serve as their assistants.
   ☐ b. as robots.
   ☐ c. to work their farms.

2. The investigator who saw a houngan dig up a coffin and raise the corpse discovered that
   ☐ a. the "corpse" had never been dead.
   ☐ b. the houngan had drugged the dead man.
   ☐ c. the "corpse" actually came back to life.

3. To keep their dead relatives from being turned into zombies, some Haitians
   ☐ a. guard the graves until the corpses have decayed.
   ☐ b. delay burying their dead for several weeks.
   ☐ c. refuse to bury their dead.

4. Voodoo originated in
   ☐ a. South America.
   ☐ b. Haiti.
   ☐ c. Africa.

5. Most investigators who have studied voodoo believe that houngans
   ☐ a. can truly raise the dead.
   ☐ b. are supernatural beings.
   ☐ c. fool people.

Score 5 points for each correct answer.

_____ **Total Score:** Recalling Facts

C | Making Inferences

When you combine your own experience and information from a text to draw a conclusion that is not directly stated in that text, you are making an inference. Below are five statements that may or may not be inferences based on information in the article. Label the statements using the following key:

C—Correct Inference   F—Faulty Inference

_____ 1. People who guard the graves of their dead have faith in the powers of the houngans.

_____ 2. Houngans believe that they have supernatural powers.

_____ 3. The element of fear plays a large role in the voodoo religion.

_____ 4. Belief in voodoo is just beginning to spread.

_____ 5. People who have been heavily drugged by houngans cannot communicate with other people.

> Score 5 points for each correct answer.
>
> _____ **Total Score:** Making Inferences

D | Using Words Precisely

Each numbered sentence below contains an underlined word or phrase from the article. Following the sentence are three definitions. One definition is closest to the meaning of the underlined word. One definition is opposite or nearly opposite. Label those two definitions using the following key. Do not label the remaining definition.

C—Closest   O—Opposite or Nearly Opposite

1. Their gaze is usually a <u>blank</u> stare, and their movements are slow and mechanical.

_____ a. foolish

_____ b. without expression

_____ c. lively

2. The mystery has never been cleared up, and some people continue to believe that voodoo is responsible for this <u>bizarre</u> occurrence.

_____ a. odd

_____ b. fortunate

_____ c. ordinary

3. Accusing him of <u>conspiring</u> with a houngan was a sure way of making trouble for him.

_____ a. acting with openness and honesty

_____ b. eating

_____ c. plotting in secret

4. Only then do they feel it is safe to end their <u>vigil</u>.

_____ a. constant watch

_____ b. life

_____ c. inattention

5. They figure that by then the corpse is too <u>decomposed</u> to be of use to any houngan who might want to turn it into a slave.

_____ a. fresh

_____ b. heavy

_____ c. decayed

_____ Score 3 points for each correct C answer.

_____ Score 2 points for each correct O answer.

_____ **Total Score:** Using Words Precisely

Enter the four total scores in the spaces below, and add them together to find your Reading Comprehension Score. Then record your score on the graph on page 197.

Score	Question Type	Lesson 18
_____	Finding the Main Idea	
_____	Recalling Facts	
_____	Making Inferences	
_____	Using Words Precisely	
_____	**Reading Comprehension Score**	

Author's Approach

Put an X in the box next to the correct answer.

1. What is the author's purpose in writing "Zombies: The Walking Dead"?

☐ a. To encourage the reader to believe in zombies

☐ b. To tell the reader about zombies and the beliefs surrounding them

☐ c. To persuade the reader that zombies don't exist

2. Choose the statement below that is the weakest argument for believing in zombies.

☐ a. A well-educated man claimed that a friend of his had been turned into a zombie.

☐ b. A woman who had died several years before showed up on a farm where people recognized her.

☐ c. Some people claim that houngans drug their victims.

3. What does the author imply by saying "Most of the stories about zombies come from poor, uneducated people"?

☐ a. Poor people tend to be more trusting than those with money.

☐ b. Poor people are natural storytellers.

☐ c. These people do not have the education necessary to question voodoo.

4. The author tells this story mainly by

☐ a. telling different stories about people who supposedly have been turned into zombies.

☐ b. comparing voodoo to drugs.

☐ c. focusing on one man's experience with houngans.

_____ Number of correct answers

Record your personal assessment of your work on the Critical Thinking Chart on page 198.

Summarizing and Paraphrasing

Follow the directions provided for questions 1 and 2. Put an X in the box next to the correct answer for question 3.

1. Look for the important ideas and events in paragraphs 10 and 11. Summarize those paragraphs in one or two sentences.

_____

_____

_____

2. Reread paragraph 5 in the article. Below, write a summary of the paragraph in no more than 25 words.

_____

_____

_____

_____

Reread your summary and decide whether it covers the important ideas in the paragraph. Next, decide how to shorten the summary to 15 words or less without leaving out any essential information. Write this summary below.

_____

_____

_____

3. Choose the best one-sentence paraphrase for the following sentence from the article:

"By believing in the houngans, the people give them power, just as a magician works real magic in the eyes of trusting and innocent children."

☐ a. Magicians are like houngans because they can turn children into zombies.

☐ b. Like trusting children, people who believe in houngans empower the voodoo priests.

☐ c. Like magicians, houngans exert their greatest influence over children.

_____ Number of correct answers

Record your personal assessment of your work on the Critical Thinking Chart on page 198.

Critical Thinking

Follow the directions provided for questions 1, 3, and 4. Put an X in the box next to the correct answer for question 2.

1. For each statement below, write O if it expresses an opinion or write F if it expresses a fact.

_____ a. Voodoo is probably the most unusual religion in the world.

_____ b. African people who were enslaved brought their voodoo religion with them to the Americas.

_____ c. Haitian burial customs have been influenced by those who believe in voodoo.

2. From the information in paragraph 12, you can predict that

☐ a. everyone in Haiti guards the graves of loved ones.

☐ b. only those who believe in voodoo guard their loved ones' graves.

☐ c. houngans can turn a decomposed corpse into a slave.

3. Choose from the letters below to correctly complete the following statement. Write the letters on the lines.

In the article, _____ and _____ are different in their ability to respond to speech.

a. normal human beings

b. robots

c. zombies

4. Read paragraph 1. Then choose from the letters below to correctly complete the following statement. Write the letters on the lines.

According to paragraph 1, _____ because _____.

a. the girls were happy to meet someone they knew

b. the girls thought that the salesgirl had been dead for three years

c. the girls were terrified

_____ Number of correct answers

Record your personal assessment of your work on the Critical Thinking Chart on page 198.

Personal Response

What new question do you have about this topic?

_____

_____

_____

_____

Self-Assessment

While reading the article, I found it easiest to

_____

_____

_____

CRITICAL THINKING

WEREWOLVES

In this 18th-century illustration, peasants attack the beast of Le Gevaudan as it claims another victim. Stories of werewolves have been around since Roman times.

In the mid 1700s, a brutal murder shook the quiet mountainous region of south-central France. There, in an isolated mountain pasture in the area known as Le Gevaudan, a young shepherd girl was found dead. That news alone was enough to shock the simple peasant families of the area. But when the cause of death was revealed, a panic spread throughout the region. The girl's heart had been torn out of her chest.

2   It turned out that the horrible murder was only the beginning. Within days, another child was killed, and then another and another. At that time, many of the children of Le Gevaudan were working as shepherds. So it was the children, alone in the mountains, who fell victim to the mad killer that became known as the Beast of Le Gevaudan.

3   Finally, after several children had been murdered, things seemed to return to normal. Weeks passed with no additional murders. The peace of the area was again shattered, however, when a peasant woman from a nearby village began spreading a frightening tale. The woman said that she had been caring for her cattle with the help

of her guard dogs, when suddenly a terrible creature appeared and began to threaten the cattle. According to the woman, the creature was as big as a donkey but walked on two legs, like a person. It was covered with short reddish hair and had a snout like a pig. It was so ferocious that the woman's dogs were terrified of it. Instead of chasing the creature away, as they were trained to do, the dogs turned and ran, leaving the woman and her cattle at the mercy of the beast. Luckily, when the monster approached the cattle, the cows lowered their horns and attacked, causing the beast to flee.

4 When the people of Le Gevaudan heard the woman's story, they weren't sure what to think. To most of them, the idea of an animal that could scare off guard dogs sounded preposterous. But their disbelief soon vanished. A local hunter known for his dependability and truthfulness reported seeing the same animal that the woman had described. The hunter explained that he had tried to shoot the creature but that his shot had done no good. He wasn't sure if he had missed or if his bullet had simply had no effect on the beast.

5 Right after the hunter reported the incident, the killings began again. More young children were found dead in the fields, their hearts torn from their bodies. The terrified people of Le Gevaudan concluded that the killer must be the monstrous creature that had been seen by the hunter and the peasant woman from the neighboring town. In desperation, the villagers announced that children would no longer be allowed to herd sheep up to the mountain pastures. Everyone also stopped going out after dark. And whenever the people of the town did gather together, they talked of nothing but the *loup-garou*, "the werewolf," that was killing their children.

6 It did not take long for stories of the loup-garou to reach the French king. He sent a detachment of soldiers to search for and destroy the beast. Almost as soon as the soldiers entered Le Gevaudan, they encountered the creature. Quickly they fired on it, but it disappeared into the woods without leaving a trace. The soldiers searched the local forests carefully, but found neither the living creature nor its body. At last the troops were convinced that they had mortally wounded the beast and that it had crawled off to some hidden place to die. The soldiers left the area, and their commander reported the success of the mission to the king.

7 The people of Le Gevaudan were delighted. They began once again to venture out after dark. The children resumed their jobs as shepherds. Everyone in the region breathed a great sigh of relief. Then, without warning, the nightmare began again. Yet another child was found dead.

8 At about the same time, an enormous wolf was spotted on a mountain in a nearby area. Again the king dispatched a band of soldiers to search for the creature. The troops did find and kill a large wolf that they claimed was the "Beast of Le Gevaudan." The king proudly announced that the loup-garou was dead. But apparently the wolf killed by the soldiers was not the loup-garou, for the killings continued. For the next three years, the monster terrorized the villagers in the area of Le Gevaudan. It left a long trail of mutilated corpses and caused many townspeople to abandon their homes and villages.

9 Finally a local nobleman decided to organize a monster hunt. The hunter, who vowed not to rest until the beast was dead, succeeded in surrounding the notorious creature in a patch of woods. One hunter fired two silver bullets at the beast, and at long last it fell dead.

10 The monster was described as a huge wolf with close-cropped ears and hooves for feet. Its carcass was carried from village to village so the people could see that the Beast of Le Gevaudan really was dead. It

This 13th-century engraving shows a wolfman who is human below the neck and wolf above.

was early summer, however, and the heat soon caused the carcass to decay. It was, therefore, necessary to bury it in a hurry. Unfortunately, the quick burial prevented people from making a full study of the creature, so today we do not have many details to help us understand what the beast looked like.

11   We do know that the people of Le Gevaudan were not the first ones to be frightened by a "werewolf." Even though it was more than 200 years ago that the Beast of Le Gevaudan terrorized the region, the idea of werewolves was an old one even then.

12   A folktale from ancient Rome tells of a young man named Niceros who had an encounter with a werewolf. One day Niceros decided to walk to another town to visit a friend. He set off with a young soldier who had offered to go along to keep him company. Soon Niceros realized that his companion was no longer walking by his side. He looked back just in time to see the soldier standing at the edge of the road, his clothes lying in a heap around his feet. As Niceros watched in horror, the soldier turned into a huge wolf and ran off into the woods.

13   Niceros was badly shaken by what he had seen, and he hurried along to his friend's house. When he arrived there, he learned that a large wolf had just killed several of his friend's sheep. The wolf had gotten away, but not before Niceros's friend had stabbed it in the neck with a spear.

14   Later, as Niceros was walking home, he passed the place where he had last seen the soldier. The clothes were gone, but the site was marked by a large pool of blood. As soon as Niceros reached his own village, he went to the home of the soldier. He found the soldier lying in bed, with a doctor bandaging a wound on his neck.

15   The story of Niceros was well-known in the Middle Ages, the period of time between 500 and 1400 A.D. During that period, many suspected werewolves were brought to trial and condemned to death. Some poor souls were executed as werewolves simply because they bore such "signs" as having hair on unusual parts of their bodies. Others were proclaimed werewolves on the basis of eyebrows that grew together in the center of their foreheads or of index fingers that were longer than their middle fingers.

16   In those dark days, it was believed that people who were in league with the devil could transform themselves into werewolves. The werewolves of the Middle Ages were pictured as regular, four-legged wolves. They were not the sort of half-man, half-wolf creature that we are familiar with from the movies. Hollywood's werewolves have given the old stories some new twists. The idea that a full moon can cause a person to turn into a werewolf is strictly from the movies. So too is the notion that a person bitten by a werewolf will turn into one himself.

17   All ideas of werewolves, it seems, grew from people's imaginations and from ancient superstitions. The earliest hunting societies often worshipped certain wild animals, which they called their totems. One group might have worshipped a bear, for instance, another a wolf. They believed that they had a special connection with the animal, perhaps even that they were descended from it. They believed that the skins of their totems had magical powers. The men would often put on the skins and perform special ceremonies involving drugs, chants, and dances. They thought that the animal's strength, power, or courage would be transmitted to them. Some of those men probably even became convinced, through the effects of a combination of drugs and their strong beliefs and desires, that they had become the animal. They would then act like the animal.

18   Given people's powers of imagination, it's not hard to see how the idea of werewolves developed from such a beginning. 🍃

If you have been timed while reading this article, enter your reading time below. Then turn to the Words-per-Minute Table on page 195 and look up your reading speed (words per minute). Enter your reading speed on the graph on page 196.

Reading Time: Lesson 19

_____ : _____

Minutes   Seconds

A | Finding the Main Idea

One statement below expresses the main idea of the article. One statement is too general, or too broad. The other statement explains only part of the article; it is too narrow. Label the statements using the following key:

M—Main Idea   **B—Too Broad**   **N—Too Narrow**

_____ 1. In the 1700s, a wild beast that the natives called the loup-garou, or werewolf, terrorized villages in the area of Le Gevaudan, France.

_____ 2. The idea of werewolves—men that turn into wolves and kill people—has been around for thousands of years.

_____ 3. People that turn into vicious wild beasts have existed in the folklore of many people for centuries.

_____ Score 15 points for a correct M answer.

_____ Score 5 points for each correct B or N answer.

_____ **Total Score:** Finding the Main Idea

B | Recalling Facts

How well do you remember the facts in the article? Put an X in the box next to the answer that correctly completes each statement about the article.

1. The Beast of Le Gevaudan killed mainly
   ☐ a. sheep.
   ☐ b. children.
   ☐ c. soldiers.

2. The soldiers who hunted the loup-garou were sent by
   ☐ a. the general of the local army.
   ☐ b. neighbors from a nearby village.
   ☐ c. the king of France.

3. When he was in the form of a wolf, the Roman soldier
   ☐ a. killed sheep.
   ☐ b. killed a number of people.
   ☐ c. attacked a man named Niceros.

4. In the Middle Ages, suspected werewolves were
   ☐ a. tried in court.
   ☐ b. executed without trials.
   ☐ c. put in cages.

5. In the myths and legends of werewolves, the beasts do not
   ☐ a. kill people or animals.
   ☐ b. enter into agreements with the devil.
   ☐ c. turn into wolves at the time of the full moon.

Score 5 points for each correct answer.

_____ **Total Score:** Recalling Facts

C | Making Inferences

When you combine your own experience and information from a text to draw a conclusion that is not directly stated in that text, you are making an inference. Below are five statements that may or may not be inferences based on information in the article. Label the statements using the following key:

C—Correct Inference   F—Faulty Inference

_____ 1. The king did not really believe that there was a loup-garou, but was just trying to calm the people.

_____ 2. Werewolves did exist in Europe in the Middle Ages.

_____ 3. During the Middle Ages, many people were suspicious and fearful of anyone who looked somewhat unusual.

_____ 4. The index fingers of most people are shorter than their middle fingers.

_____ 5. The people of Le Gevaudan stopped herding sheep during the years in which the loup-garou was on the loose.

Score 5 points for each correct answer.

_____ **Total Score:** Making Inferences

D | Using Words Precisely

Each numbered sentence below contains an underlined word or phrase from the article. Following the sentence are three definitions. One definition is closest to the meaning of the underlined word. One definition is opposite or nearly opposite. Label those two definitions using the following key. Do not label the remaining definition.

C—Closest   O—Opposite or Nearly Opposite

1. To most of them, the idea of an animal that could scare off guard dogs sounded <u>preposterous</u>.

_____ a. sensible

_____ b. loud

_____ c. absurd

2. At last the troops were convinced that they had <u>mortally</u> wounded the beast and that it had crawled off to some hidden place to die.

_____ a. fatally

_____ b. not seriously

_____ c. finally

3. The idea that a full moon can cause a person to turn into a werewolf is <u>strictly</u> from the movies.

_____ a. fortunately

_____ b. solely

_____ c. partly

4. In those dark days, it was believed that people who were <u>in league with</u> the devil could turn themselves into werewolves.

_____ a. separated from

_____ b. similar to

_____ c. united with

5. Others were <u>proclaimed</u> werewolves on the basis of eyebrows that grew together or of index fingers that were longer than their middle fingers.

_____ a. not said to be

_____ b. declared to be

_____ c. fed to

_____ Score 3 points for each correct C answer.

_____ Score 2 points for each correct O answer.

_____ **Total Score:** Using Words Precisely

Enter the four total scores in the spaces below, and add them together to find your Reading Comprehension Score. Then record your score on the graph on page 197.

Score	Question Type	Lesson 19
_____	Finding the Main Idea	
_____	Recalling Facts	
_____	Making Inferences	
_____	Using Words Precisely	
_____	**Reading Comprehension Score**	

Author's Approach

Put an X in the box next to the correct answer.

1. The author uses the first sentence of the article to

☐ a. inform the reader when and where a brutal murder took place.

☐ b. describe the qualities of werewolves.

☐ c. entertain the reader with a monster story.

2. What does the author mean by the statement "Others were proclaimed werewolves on the basis of eyebrows that grew together in the center of their foreheads or of index fingers that were longer than their middle fingers"?

☐ a. People with very thick eyebrows or long fingers admitted to being werewolves.

☐ b. Werewolves had very long fingers.

☐ c. These slight physical abnormalities were considered signs of being a werewolf.

3. Choose the statement below that best describes the author's position in paragraph 17.

☐ a. People in early hunting societies were in league with the devil.

☐ b. The notion of werewolves sprung from people's imaginations and superstitions.

☐ c. People in early hunting societies worshipped werewolves.

4. The author probably wrote this article in order to

☐ a. convince the reader that werewolves really existed in France.

☐ b. frighten the reader.

☐ c. explain how the idea of werewolves developed.

_____ Number of correct answers

Record your personal assessment of your work on the Critical Thinking Chart on page 198.

Summarizing and Paraphrasing

Follow the directions provided for question 1. Put an X in the box next to the correct answer for question 2.

1. Complete the following one-sentence summary of the article using the lettered phrases from the phrase bank below. Write the letters on the lines.

> **Phrase Bank:**
>
> a. the story of the Beast of Le Gevaudan
>
> b. the theory that werewolves developed as a result of people's imaginations
>
> c. earlier tales and the treatment of supposed werewolves

The article about werewolves begins with _____, goes on to explain _____, and ends with _____.

2. Choose the sentence that correctly restates the following sentence from the article:

"Instead of chasing the creature away, as they were trained to do, the dogs turned and ran, leaving the woman and her cattle at the mercy of the beast."

☐ a. Instead of chasing the creature, the dogs attacked the woman and her cattle.

☐ b. The beast showed the woman and her cattle mercy when the dogs turned and ran away.

☐ c. In spite of their training, the dogs ran away, leaving the woman and her cattle to fight the werewolf alone.

> _____ Number of correct answers
>
> Record your personal assessment of your work on the Critical Thinking Chart on page 74.

Critical Thinking

Put an X in the box next to the correct answer for questions 1, 3, and 4. Follow the directions provided for the other questions.

1. From the article, you can predict that if people had been able to study the corpse of the Beast of Le Gevaudan more thoroughly,

☐ a. we would have a better idea of what the creature looked like.

☐ b. people would believe in werewolves today.

☐ c. movies about werewolves would never have been made.

2. Choose from the letters below to correctly complete the following statement. Write the letters on the lines.

In the article, _____ and _____ are alike.

a. the creature that Niceros saw

b. the creature that a peasant woman saw

c. the creature that a hunter saw

3. What was the effect of the murderous attacks on children tending sheep in Le Gevaudan?

☐ a. Everyone in the region breathed a sigh of relief.

☐ b. Children were no longer allowed to herd sheep in the mountains.

☐ c. The children resumed their jobs as shepherds.

4. If you were a leader, how could you use the information in the article to quiet people's fears about a killer beast on the loose?

☐ a. Encourage people to stay indoors after dark.

☐ b. Put on animal skins and perform special ceremonies.

☐ c. Send out hunters to track down and kill the beast.

5. Which paragraphs from the article provide evidence that supports your answer to question 2?

_____

_____

_____ Number of correct answers

Record your personal assessment of your work on the Critical Thinking Chart on page 198.

Personal Response

I disagree with the author because

_____

_____

_____

_____

The part I found most difficult about the article was

_____

_____

_____

_____

I found this difficult because

_____

_____

_____

_____

THE MOKELE-MBEMBE
Are All the Dinosaurs Gone?

This illustration of a water monster seen in the African Congo is based on eyewitness descriptions.

The last of the dinosaurs vanished about 65 million years ago. They were wiped out in some cataclysmic event. Everyone agrees about that, right? Well, it turns out that not everyone is so sure that *all* the dinosaurs disappeared. For many years, the native peoples of equatorial Africa have reported seeing some sort of weird creature that looks very much like a small version of a brontosaurus.

2   Could it be that dinosaurs still walk the earth in a remote part of the world? Could they have found ways to adapt to the arrival of new competitors in the food chain? If so, tropical Africa is the most likely place for them to reside because it is one of the few spots on Earth that totally escaped the changes wrought by the great ice ages. For that reason, tropical Africa looks pretty much as it did 65 million years ago.

3   This region has only been explored during the past 150 years or so. Could the explorers have missed something? By now, of course, almost every mile of Africa has been examined. And with each

passing year, the odds of any strange or unknown creature surviving undetected grow slimmer.

4   Still, in the remote regions of what are now the Congo and Gabon, reports persist of a dinosaurlike monster. These reports go back at least 200 years. Some appear in old European books and journals. In 1913, for instance, a German explorer named Freiherr Von Stein summarized several sightings of a beast that the pygmies call *Mokele-Mbembe*, which means "monstrous animal." The explorer wrote: "The animal is said to be a brownish-grey color with smooth skin, its size approximately that of an elephant…. It is said to have a very long and flexible neck and only one tooth but a very long one. A few spoke about a long muscular tail like that of an alligator. Canoes coming near it are said to be doomed, the animal [kills] the crews but without eating the bodies."

5   In 1979 an expedition set out to look for Mokele-Mbembe. Its leader was a zoologist named James Powell. Like a police officer looking for a criminal suspect, he showed local people pictures of a sauropod, a plant-eating dinosaur that looks somewhat like a brontosaurus. Many villagers recognized the creature, but they called it N'yamala. They said that it lived in the deep swamps of Gabon.

They added that it had blood-red eyes, a huge mouth, and one tooth.

6   A witch doctor told Powell that he had seen the animal himself many years ago. He described it as being mostly neck and tail, more than 30 feet long, and at least as heavy as an elephant. After studying the record, Powell concluded that N'yamala was the same creature as Mokele-Mbembe. Although he reported many sightings by native peoples, Powell never saw the beast for himself.

7   In 1981, an American named Herman Regusters went looking for Mokele-Mbembe. He reached Lake Tele where most of the sightings occurred. Quite possibly, Regusters was the first outsider to see this small round lake in the Congo. He also became the first Westerner to claim he saw the monster. He gathered sound recordings, plaster-cast footprints, and samples of droppings. Regusters even took pictures of the beast, but the prints turned out foggy and unclear.

8   The next search, in 1983, was led by Marcellin

Agnagna, a zoologist from the Congo's Brazzaville Zoo. He, too, reported seeing Mokele-Mbembe at Lake Tele. Agnagna claimed that the animal was in the lake about 300 yards from shore. He described the creature as a reptile about 16 feet long with a thin reddish head, oval eyes like a crocodile, a long neck, and a broad black back.

9   Since then there have been at least three other expeditions to find Mokele-

Herman Regusters points to the Lake Tele area of the Republic of the Congo, where there have been sightings of the mokele-mbemba.

Mbembe. None of these has resulted in more sightings, however. One Japanese group claimed that the animal probably doesn't live in Lake Tele. Instead, they say, Mokele-Mbembe lives in the *molibos*, the small jungle streams that flow into the lake.

10   Others are not so convinced that Mokele-Mbembe exists at all. In his 1997 book *No Mercy*, travel writer Redmond O'Hanlon tells about his search to find the mysterious African dinosaur. With him went Marcellin Agnagna. Agnagna's grandfather gave both men good luck charms to protect them from evil spirits at Lake Tele. O'Hanlon thought he would need these talismans because another native man predicted that he would die a "long, messy, mutilated death" at Lake Tele.

11   O'Hanlon did not die, but he did become very sick. During his illness, he had wild, bizarre dreams. When at last he emerged from the jungle, he was weak, filthy, and totally exhausted. As for the Mokele-Mbembe, O'Hanlon was convinced that the eyewitnesses had seen nothing more than forest elephants crossing the lake with their trunks raised. Another theory is that the "dinosaur" is really a python. Pythons are not true water snakes; they swim with their heads above the water's surface. The rest of their bodies trail behind making bumps in the water.

12   Perhaps, though, O'Hanlon and other skeptics are wrong. Perhaps the Mokele-Mbembe is just too elusive to be caught, and the Age of the Dinosaurs isn't really over after all. 🍃

If you have been timed while reading this article, enter your reading time below. Then turn to the Words-per-Minute Table on page 195 and look up your reading speed (words per minute). Enter your reading speed on the graph on page 196.

Reading Time: **Lesson 20**

_____ : _____
Minutes   Seconds

A | Finding the Main Idea

One statement below expresses the main idea of the article. One statement is too general, or too broad. The other statement explains only part of the article; it is too narrow. Label the statements using the following key:

M—Main Idea   **B—Too Broad**   **N—Too Narrow**

_____ 1. A dinosaur known as Mokele-Mbembe is said to live in remote regions of equatorial Africa.

_____ 2. American explorer Herman Regusters was the first Westerner to see Mokele-Mbembe.

_____ 3. Tropical Africa is the most likely place for dinosaurs to live today because the region escaped the changes brought about by the great ice ages.

_____ Score 15 points for a correct M answer.

_____ Score 5 points for each correct B or N answer.

_____ **Total Score:** Finding the Main Idea

B | Recalling Facts

How well do you remember the facts in the article? Put an X in the box next to the answer that correctly completes each statement about the article.

1. The pygmy term *Mokele-Mbembe* means
   - ☐ a. "brontosaurus."
   - ☐ b. "dinosaur."
   - ☐ c. "monstrous animal."

2. The German explorer who wrote about the beast in 1913 was
   - ☐ a. Freiherr Von Stein.
   - ☐ b. James Powell.
   - ☐ c. Marcellin Agnagna.

3. Both Regusters and Agnagna saw Mokele-Mbembe
   - ☐ a. in Gabon.
   - ☐ b. in Brazzaville.
   - ☐ c. at Lake Tele.

4. During Redmond O'Hanlon's search to find the African dinosaur, he
   - ☐ a. became very sick.
   - ☐ b. died a long, messy death.
   - ☐ c. took pictures of Mokele-Mbembe.

5. O'Hanlon believes that people claiming to have seen the Mokele-Mbembe actually saw
   - ☐ a. a python.
   - ☐ b. an elephant.
   - ☐ c. an alligator.

Score 5 points for each correct answer.

_____ **Total Score:** Recalling Facts

C | Making Inferences

When you combine your own experience and information from a text to draw a conclusion that is not directly stated in that text, you are making an inference. Below are five statements that may or may not be inferences based on information in the article. Label the statements using the following key:

C—Correct Inference   **F—Faulty Inference**

_____ 1. Dinosaurs could not have survived in North America.

_____ 2. Mokele-Mbembe hunts and kills people for food.

_____ 3. Many villagers in equatorial Africa believe that Mokele-Mbembe exists.

_____ 4. Mokele-Mbembe cannot swim.

_____ 5. Freiherr Von Stein saw the mysterious African dinosaur.

Score 5 points for each correct answer.

_____ **Total Score:** Making Inferences

D | Using Words Precisely

Each numbered sentence below contains an underlined word or phrase from the article. Following the sentence are three definitions. One definition is closest to the meaning of the underlined word. One definition is opposite or nearly opposite. Label those two definitions using the following key. Do not label the remaining definition.

C—Closest   **O—Opposite or Nearly Opposite**

1. They were wiped out in some <u>cataclysmic</u> event.

_____ a. disastrous

_____ b. modern

_____ c. beneficial

2. Could they have found ways to <u>adapt to</u> the arrival of new competitors in the food chain?

_____ a. predict

_____ b. die as a result of

_____ c. adjust to

3. If so, tropical Africa is the most likely place for them to reside because it is one of the few spots on Earth that totally escaped the changes <u>wrought</u> by the great ice ages.

_____ a. frozen

_____ b. brought about

_____ c. prevented

4. "It is said to have a very long and <u>flexible</u> neck and only one tooth but a very long one."

_____ a. peculiar

_____ b. rigid

_____ c. elastic

5. O'Hanlon thought he would need his because another native man predicted that he would die a "long, messy, <u>mutilated</u> death" at Lake Tele.

_____ a. disfigured

_____ b. unblemished

_____ c. undisturbed

_____ Score 3 points for each correct C answer.

_____ Score 2 points for each correct O answer.

_____ **Total Score:** Using Words Precisely

Enter the four total scores in the spaces below, and add them together to find your Reading Comprehension Score. Then record your score on the graph on page 197.

Score	Question Type	Lesson 20
_____	Finding the Main Idea	
_____	Recalling Facts	
_____	Making Inferences	
_____	Using Words Precisely	
_____	**Reading Comprehension Score**	

Author's Approach

Put an X in the box next to the correct answer.

1. What is the author's purpose in writing "The Mokele-Mbembe: Are All the Dinosaurs Really Dead?"

☐ a. To tell the reader about the attempts to find a dinosaurlike monster reportedly seen in equatorial Africa

☐ b. To describe equatorial Africa

☐ c. To emphasize the similarities between the African dinosaur and an elephant

2. From the statement "Like a police officer looking for a criminal suspect, he [James Powell] showed local people pictures of a sauropod, a plant-eating dinosaur that looks somewhat like a brontosaurus," you can conclude that the author wants the reader to think that Powell was

☐ a. sure that the local people hadn't seen the monster.

☐ b. prepared to arrest the monster.

☐ c. carrying out a very thorough exploration for the monster.

3. How is the author's purpose for writing the article expressed in paragraph 7?

☐ a. The author describes Lake Tele in the Congo.

☐ b. The author compares the Mokele-Mbembe's footprints with those of other animals.

☐ c. The author informs the reader about Herman Regusters's efforts to find the Mokele-Mbembe.

_____ Number of correct answers

Record your personal assessment of your work on the Critical Thinking Chart on page 198.

Summarizing and Paraphrasing

Follow the directions provided for questions 1 and 2. Put an X in the box next to the correct answer for question 3.

1. Complete the following one-sentence summary of the article using the lettered phrases from the phrase bank below. Write the letters on the lines.

> **Phrase Bank:**
> a. early reports of the monster in Africa
> b. theories about the "dinosaur"
> c. recent expeditions undertaken to search for the beast

After a short introduction, the article about the Mokele-Mbembe discusses _____, goes on to explain _____, and ends with _____.

2. Reread paragraph 7 in the article. Below, write a summary of the paragraph in no more than 25 words.

_____

_____

_____

_____

Reread your summary and decide whether it covers the important ideas in the paragraph. Next, decide how to shorten the summary to 15 words or less without leaving out any essential information. Write this summary below.

_____

_____

3. Choose the sentence that correctly restates the following sentence from the article:
    "As for the Mokele-Mbembe, O'Hanlon was convinced that the eyewitnesses had seen nothing more than forest elephants crossing the lake with their trunks raised."

☐ a. O'Hanlon mistook elephants crossing the lake with raised trunks for the Mokele-Mbembe.

☐ b. O'Hanlon thought that those claiming to have seen the Mokele-Mbembe in the lake had actually seen elephants with raised trunks.

☐ c. The eyewitnesses told O'Hanlon that they had seen elephants with raised trunks and not the Mokele-Mbembe.

> _____ Number of correct answers
>
> Record your personal assessment of your work on the Critical Thinking Chart on page 198.

Critical Thinking

Put an X in the box next to the correct answer for questions 1, 2, and 5. Follow the directions provided for the other questions.

1. Which of the following statements from the article is an opinion rather than a fact?

☐ a. "Perhaps the Mokele-Mbembe is just too elusive to be caught, and the Age of the Dinosaurs isn't really over after all."

☐ b. "For that reason, tropical Africa looks pretty much as it did 65 million years ago."

☐ c. "Pythons are not true water snakes; they swim with their head above the water's surface."

2. From what the article told about Marcellin Agnagna's first expedition, you can predict that he would

☐ a. not agree with O'Hanlon's theory about the Mokele-Mbembe.

☐ b. agree with O'Hanlon's theory about the Mokele-Mbembe.

☐ c. throw away his good luck charm after completing his expedition with O'Hanlon.

3. Choose from the letters below to correctly complete the following statement. Write the letters on the lines.

In the article, _____ and _____ are most alike.

a. the monster known as the Mokele-Mbembe

b. the monster known as the N'yamala

c. the monster known as the python

4. Read paragraph 11. Then choose from the letters below to correctly complete the following statement. Write the letters on the lines.

According to paragraph 11, _____ because _____.

a. he became very sick

b. he emerged from the jungle

c. O'Hanlon had bizarre dreams

5. What did you have to do to answer question 4?

☐ a. find an opinion (what someone thinks about something)

☐ b. find a cause (why something happened)

☐ c. draw a conclusion (a sensible statement based on the text and your experience)

_____ Number of correct answers

Record your personal assessment of your work on the Critical Thinking Chart on page 198.

Personal Response

A question I would like answered by Redmond O'Hanlon is

_____

_____

_____

_____

Self-Assessment

Which concepts or ideas from the article were difficult to understand?

_____

_____

_____

_____

Which were easy to understand?

_____

_____

_____

_____

DRAGONS

This dragon illustration is from a handwritten treatise on alchemy from the 17th century.

Everyone has an idea of what dragons look like. We have seen illustrations of them. We have seen them in movies. We have read descriptions of them. Dragons are huge beasts, housetop high when they rear up. They have long, barbed tails. Smoke belches from their flaring nostrils. They exhale sheets of flame from mouths rimmed with daggerlike teeth. Their legs end in terrible long claws. Scaly armor glistens on their tough hides, and batlike wings project from their backs. Sometimes they even have more than one head! Many dragons also have the magical ability to change size at will, or to disappear.

2   In folktales and in fairy tales, dragons often terrorize the countryside. They swoop down from their mountain caves and incinerate villages and crops with their fiery breath. They carry away innocent people and strike terror into the hearts of all but the boldest. Kings, queens, and mayors call upon brave knights or clever young people to slay the dreadful beasts and restore peace.

3   Since ancient times, there have been legends of dragons. People long ago lived in fear that they might be lurking just over the horizon, out there in the next mountain range, or just over the edge of the ocean, where the earth ends. Mapmakers of long ago decorated the areas around what they believed to be a flat earth with colorful drawings of dragons. Not even the most adventuresome folk wanted to reach that point in their travels. Seamen swore that they saw steam from the breath of the beasts, far out over the billowing waves. Hunters frequently saw them circling in the air above distant peaks

and saw their eyes glowing in the dark just outside the circle of campfire light.

4   There was no doubt in anyone's mind that dragons existed—somewhere. The Bible mentions dragons several times. The myths and folktales of ancient Britain and Europe are filled with dragons. Stories from the East featured dragons, although the Chinese dragons were of a more peaceful sort than those of the West. Surprisingly, there was general agreement about the appearance and habits of the creatures.

5   Wherever people believed in dragons, however, it's generally safe to say that the wise folk were just as happy to think that the creatures were far away, minding their own business. The more adventurous sort, of course, liked the thought that if they were lucky and brave enough, maybe they would meet and conquer a dragon and, in the process, win their king's favor. Perhaps they would even get to claim the golden treasure hoard that dragons were always rumored to be hiding and guarding.

6   One of the best-known dragons in all of literature is the terrible Smaug in J. R. R. Tolkien's popular fantasy novel *The Hobbit*. At one point in the story, the hero, a timid little "hobbit" named Bilbo Baggins, fearfully approaches the great Smaug in his lair. Even before he sees "The Great Worm," Bilbo can hear him—a throbbing sound, "a sort of bubbling like the noise of a large pot galloping on the fire, mixed with the rumble of a giant tomcat purring." Suddenly, around a turn, there is Smaug:

Smaug lay, with wings folded like an immeasurable bat, turned partly on one side so that the hobbit could see his underparts and his long pale belly crusted with gems and fragments of gold from his long lying on his costly bed. Behind him where the walls were nearest could dimly be seen coats of mail, helms and axes, swords and spears and vessels filled with a wealth that could not be guessed.

7   In a later passage Smaug describes himself in this way:

My armour is like tenfold shields, my teeth are swords, my claws spears, and the shock of my tail a thunderbolt, my wings a hurricane, and my breath death!

8   Smaug possesses many of the characteristics for which dragons have traditionally been known. But dragons are, of course, make-believe. How is it, then, that people all over the world seem to be in fairly close agreement on what they look like and how they behave?

9   Well, descriptions of dragons sound very much like descriptions of pterodactyls—the giant, leathery, featherless ancestors of birds. It seems to make sense that dragons would be based on the human race's memories of dinosaurs. Those giant prehistoric creatures certainly share many of the reptilian features we associate with dragons. This theory breaks down, however, when we consider that the Age of Dinosaurs ended 65 million years before there were humans on earth.

Draco volans, *found in the Malay Islands, use their winglike membranes to "fly" from tree to tree.*

10   It's more likely that our ideas about dragons are based on some poor descriptions and pictures of present-day reptiles. We know that the term *dragon* is related to reptiles. It comes from the ancient Roman word *draco*, which was the name of a tree-dwelling snake said to drop from branches onto people and animals passing beneath. Those creatures swallowed their prey whole. It's probable that the draco was a giant python.

11   There are other ordinary creatures that also have characteristics that we associate with dragons. Crocodiles, for instance, have terrible teeth, bent legs, and thick hides. Those body parts look much like the teeth, legs, and armored hide of a dragon. People who first heard about crocodiles from someone who had seen one must have pictured a terrible creature indeed.

12   Even the dragon's fiery breath has a surprising parallel in the world of reptiles. The Indian cobra can spit its deadly venom as far as 10 feet, blinding any victim whose eyes it reaches. It's not hard to imagine a blind traveler swearing that "the beast shot flames into my eyes and burned them out." Also, if you've ever seen a picture of a cobra drawing itself upright into position to strike, with its hood spread wide behind its frightening face, you know how easily the quick glance of a terrified person could see the wide-spread hood as wings that had lifted the creature above the ground.

13   Even descriptions of dragons as great flying snakes have their basis in a real creature. It is called the Draco volans. This large lizard is found in the Malay Islands. It has winglike membranes that stretch between its front and rear legs. It can leap from a limb, and by stretching its legs wide to spread the membranes, glide to another tree. It can glide for distances of up to 40 feet.

14   You can see how such creatures grew to terrible proportions in the minds of people of long ago who were unfamiliar with them. But though in the lands of the West dragons are terrible beasts, in the East they are usually harmless, and even good and helpful.

15   The dragons of China and Japan are longer and more snakelike than those of the West. Modern dragon experts Paul and Karin Jobsgard describe the Asian dragon this way: "a head like a camel's, horns like a deer's, eyes like a hare's, ears like a bull's, a neck like an iguana's, a belly like a frog's, scales like a carp's, paws like a tiger's, and claws like an eagle's. The long, tendril-like whiskers extending from either side of its mouth are probably used in feeling its way along the bottom of muddy ponds. Its color varies from greenish to golden, with a series of alternating short and long spines extending down the back and along the tail, where they become longer."

16   Chinese historians record that there are traditionally nine types of Chinese dragons including the primitive *k'uei dragon* from which all others evolved. The advanced species are the horned dragon, the winged dragon, the celestial dragon (which supports and protects the mansions of the gods), the spiritual dragon (which makes wind and rain), the dragon of hidden treasures (which keeps guard over concealed wealth), the coiling dragon (which lives in water), the yellow dragon (which once emerged from water and presented the legendary Emperor Fu Hsi with the elements of writing), and the dragon king, which is actually four separate creatures, each of which rules over one of the four points of the compass.

17   Such are the main facts about some of history's and literature's dragons. We know they don't exist, and we think we can explain how everyone came to agree on precisely what a nonexistent creature looked like. We can even understand how some people really could believe they had seen a dragon. Our imaginations are very good at assembling parts of things we *have* seen or heard about into something we *think* we have seen. There really is a rational explanation for the terrible mythical figure of the dragon. But that doesn't stop some of us from still hoping that perhaps somewhere, in a cave or on a mountain peak... 🍂

If you have been timed while reading this article, enter your reading time below. Then turn to the Words-per-Minute Table on page 195 and look up your reading speed (words per minute). Enter your reading speed on the graph on page 196.

Reading Time: Lesson 21

_____ : _____
Minutes   Seconds

A | Finding the Main Idea

One statement below expresses the main idea of the article. One statement is too general, or too broad. The other statement explains only part of the article; it is too narrow. Label the statements using the following key:

M—Main Idea   **B—Too Broad**   **N—Too Narrow**

_____ 1. Dragons have lived in myths and legends for ages, and many of their characteristics are similar to physical features and habits of some real creatures.

_____ 2. Though dragons lived only in stories and in people's imaginations, the beasts seem to have some relation to reality.

_____ 3. Western dragons are terrible, evil beasts, but those of the East are usually good and peaceful.

_____ Score 15 points for a correct M answer.

_____ Score 5 points for each correct B or N answer.

_____ **Total Score:** Finding the Main Idea

B | Recalling Facts

How well do you remember the facts in the article? Put an X in the box next to the answer that correctly completes each statement about the article.

1. Long ago, when people thought that the earth was flat, they believed that dragons lived
   - ☐ a. in the zoo.
   - ☐ b. in caves.
   - ☐ c. just over the edges of the earth.

2. The term *dragon* is related to
   - ☐ a. reptiles.
   - ☐ b. birds.
   - ☐ c. mammals.

3. The *draco*, which dropped from trees and swallowed their prey whole were probably
   - ☐ a. king cobras.
   - ☐ b. giant pythons.
   - ☐ c. flying lizards.

4. The hood of a cobra poised to strike may have been the basis for a dragon's
   - ☐ a. great teeth.
   - ☐ b. venom.
   - ☐ c. wings.

5. How many traditional types of Chinese dragons are there?
   - ☐ a. nine
   - ☐ b. thirteen
   - ☐ c. seven

Score 5 points for each correct answer.

_____ **Total Score:** Recalling Facts

C **Making Inferences**

When you combine your own experience and information from a text to draw a conclusion that is not directly stated in that text, you are making an inference. Below are five statements that may or may not be inferences based on information in the article. Label the statements using the following key:

C—Correct Inference   **F—Faulty Inference**

_____ 1. There are no evil monsters in Chinese myths and legends.

_____ 2. It is likely that some types of dragons did exist around the time of the dinosaurs.

_____ 3. The idea of dragons grew up from people's fears of things that they did not understand.

_____ 4. Dragons stole the treasure that they guard in their lairs.

_____ 5. Dragon worship was part of many ancient religious ceremonies.

Score 5 points for each correct answer.

_____ **Total Score:** Making Inferences

D **Using Words Precisely**

Each numbered sentence below contains an underlined word or phrase from the article. Following the sentence are three definitions. One definition is closest to the meaning of the underlined word. One definition is opposite or nearly opposite. Label those two definitions using the following key. Do not label the remaining definition.

C—Closest   O—Opposite or Nearly Opposite

1. They swoop down from their mountain caves and <u>incinerate</u> villages and crops with their fiery breath.

    _____ a. burn to ashes

    _____ b. put out a fire

    _____ c. flatten

2. Even the dragon's fiery breath has a surprising <u>parallel</u> in the world of reptiles.

    _____ a. friend

    _____ b. opposite

    _____ c. equal

3. Chinese historians record that there are traditionally nine types of Chinese dragons, including the primitive *k'uei dragon*, from which all others <u>evolved</u>.

    _____ a. died out

    _____ b. stole

    _____ c. developed

4. There really is a <u>rational</u> explanation for the terrible mythical figure of the dragon.

_____ a. reasonable

_____ b. senseless

_____ c. fascinating

5. Also, if you've ever seen a picture of a cobra <u>drawing</u> itself upright into a position to strike, you know how easily the quick glance of a terrified person could see the widespread hood as wings that had lifted the creature above the ground.

_____ a. pulling

_____ b. contorting

_____ c. pushing

_____ Score 3 points for each correct C answer.

_____ Score 2 points for each correct O answer.

_____ **Total Score:** Using Words Precisely

Enter the four total scores in the spaces below, and add them together to find your Reading Comprehension Score. Then record your score on the graph on page 197.

Score	Question Type	Lesson 21
_____	Finding the Main Idea	
_____	Recalling Facts	
_____	Making Inferences	
_____	Using Words Precisely	
_____	**Reading Comprehension Score**	

Author's Approach

Put an X in the box next to the correct answer.

1. Which of the following statements from the article best describes the activities of Western dragons?

☐ a. "They swoop down from their mountain caves and incinerate villages and crops with their fiery breath. They carry away beautiful maidens and strike terror into the hearts of all but the boldest."

☐ b. "'A head like a camel's, horns like a deer's, eyes like a hare's, ears like a bull's, a neck like an iguana's, a belly like a frog's, scales like a carp's, paws like a tiger's, and claws like an eagle's.'"

☐ c. "It can leap from a limb, and by stretching its legs wide to spread the membranes, glide to another tree."

2. From the statement "But that doesn't stop some of us from still hoping that perhaps somewhere, in a cave or on a mountain peak…," you can conclude that the author wants the reader to think that some people

☐ a. actually believe in dragons.

☐ b. have seen dragons in a cave or on a mountain peak.

☐ c. enjoy thinking about make-believe dragons.

3. Choose the statement below that is the weakest argument for claiming that dragons are based on descriptions of pterodactyls.

☐ a. The prehistoric creatures share many of the dragon's reptilian features.

☐ b. Dragons and pterodactyls can both fly.

☐ c. The Age of Dinosaurs ended 65 million years before there were humans on Earth.

4. Choose the statement below that best describes the author's position in paragraph 17.

☐ a. The author believes that dragons really can be found in a cave or on a mountain peak.

☐ b. The author says that no one really understands how we developed our ideas of what dragons look like.

☐ c. The author claims that there is a rational explanation for the mythical figure of a dragon.

_____ Number of correct answers

Record your personal assessment of your work on the Critical Thinking Chart on page 198.

Summarizing and Paraphrasing

Follow the directions provided for question 1. Put an X in the box next to the correct answer for question 2.

1. Reread paragraph 12 in the article. Below, write a summary of the paragraph in no more than 25 words.

_____

_____

_____

_____

Reread your summary and decide whether it covers the important ideas in the paragraph. Next, decide how to shorten the summary to 15 words or less without leaving out any essential information. Write this summary below.

_____

_____

2. Choose the sentence that correctly restates the following sentences from the article:

"The more adventurous sort, of course, liked the thought that if they were lucky and brave enough, maybe they would meet and conquer a dragon and, in the process, win their king's favor. Perhaps they would even get to claim the golden treasure hoard that dragons were always rumored to be hiding and guarding."

☐ a. The most adventuresome hoped to defeat a dragon and, in the process, impress the king or take the dragon's treasure.

☐ b. Some of the more adventuresome wanted to meet a dragon and then steal its servant or its treasure.

☐ c. The most adventuresome hoped to challenge a dragon to a game and then try to win favors from the king or else a great treasure.

_____ Number of correct answers

Record your personal assessment of your work on the Critical Thinking Chart on page 198.

Critical Thinking

Put an X in the box next to the correct answer for questions 1, 3, and 4. Follow the directions provided for the other questions.

1. From what the article told about Smaug, you can predict that the dragon would

☐ a. offer to share his gems and gold with any visitor.

☐ b. purr like a cat if anyone tried to take his treasure.

☐ c. fight Bilbo Baggins or anyone else who tried to take his treasure.

CRITICAL THINKING

2. Choose from the letters below to correctly complete the following statement. Write the letters on the lines.

In the article, _____ and _____ are different.

a. dragons in the East

b. Smaug

c. dragons in the West

3. What was the cause of a seaman's reluctance to sail over the edge of the earth?

☐ a. Mapmakers decorated their maps with colorful drawings.

☐ b. People believed that dragons lurked just over the edge of the ocean.

☐ c. People believed that the earth was round.

4. How is a dragon an example of a monster?

☐ a. Dragons are related to crocodiles, snakes, and other reptiles.

☐ b. A dragon is a huge fire-breathing beast that was believed to terrorize countrysides and lurk on the edge of the world.

☐ c. Dragons are mentioned in the Bible and in many myths and folktales.

5. In which paragraph did you find the information or details to answer question 3?

_____

_____ Number of correct answers

Record your personal assessment of your work on the Critical Thinking Chart on page 198.

Personal Response

Would you recommend this article to other students? Explain.

_____

_____

_____

_____

Self-Assessment

A word or phrase in the article that I do not understand is

_____

_____

_____

_____

Compare and Contrast

Think about the articles you read in Unit Three. Choose the four monsters that you feel are most memorable. Write the titles of the articles that tell about them in the first column of the chart below. Use information from the articles to fill in the empty boxes in the chart.

Title	Which part of the article would you be most likely to retell to friends?	Which aspects of the article are most believable, if any?	Why have people reacted strongly to this monster? Which fears does this monster provoke?

Which monster would you most like to see in a movie? _____ Describe three other characters who would appear in the movie

and how they would help conquer the monster or become its victims _____

Words-per-Minute Table

Unit Three

Directions: If you were timed while reading an article, refer to the Reading Time you recorded in the box at the end of the article. Use this words-per-minute table to determine your reading speed for that article. Then plot your reading speed on the graph on page 196.

Lesson / No. of Words	15 / 1229	16 / 1043	17 / 939	18 / 1091	19 / 1519	20 / 872	21 / 1467	Seconds
1:30	819	695	626	727	1013	581	978	90
1:40	737	626	563	655	911	523	880	100
1:50	670	569	512	595	829	476	800	110
2:00	615	522	470	546	760	436	734	120
2:10	567	481	433	504	701	402	677	130
2:20	527	447	402	468	651	374	629	140
2:30	492	417	376	436	608	349	587	150
2:40	461	391	352	409	570	327	550	160
2:50	434	368	331	385	536	308	518	170
3:00	410	348	313	364	506	291	489	180
3:10	388	329	297	345	480	275	463	190
3:20	369	313	282	327	456	262	440	200
3:30	351	298	268	312	434	249	419	210
3:40	335	284	256	298	414	238	400	220
3:50	321	272	245	285	396	227	383	230
4:00	307	261	235	273	380	218	367	240
4:10	295	250	225	262	365	209	352	250
4:20	284	241	217	252	351	201	339	260
4:30	273	232	209	242	338	194	326	270
4:40	263	224	201	234	326	187	314	280
4:50	254	216	194	226	314	180	304	290
5:00	246	209	188	218	304	174	293	300
5:10	238	202	182	211	294	169	284	310
5:20	230	196	176	205	285	164	275	320
5:30	223	190	171	198	276	159	267	330
5:40	217	184	166	193	268	154	259	340
5:50	211	179	161	187	260	149	251	350
6:00	205	174	157	182	253	145	245	360
6:10	199	169	152	177	246	141	238	370
6:20	194	165	148	172	240	138	232	380
6:30	189	160	144	168	234	134	226	390
6:40	184	156	141	164	228	131	220	400
6:50	180	153	137	160	222	128	215	410
7:00	176	149	134	156	217	125	210	420
7:10	171	146	131	152	212	122	205	430
7:20	168	142	128	149	207	119	200	440
7:30	164	139	125	145	203	116	196	450
7:40	160	136	122	142	198	114	191	460
7:50	157	133	120	139	194	111	187	470
8:00	154	130	117	136	190	109	183	480

Minutes and Seconds

Plotting Your Progress: Reading Speed

Unit Three

Directions: If you were timed while reading an article, write your words-per-minute rate for that in the box under the number of the lesson. Then plot your reading speed on the graph by putting a small X on the line directly above the number of the lesson, across from the number of words per minute you read. As you mark your speed for each lesson, graph your progress by drawing a line to connect the X's.

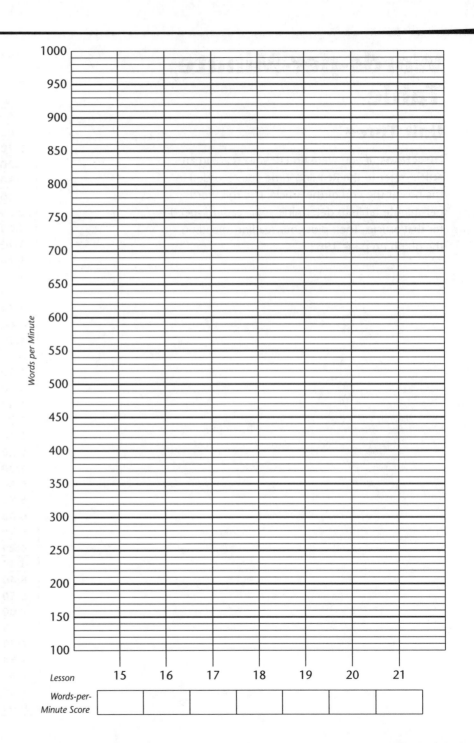

Lesson	15	16	17	18	19	20	21
Words-per-Minute Score							

Plotting Your Progress: Reading Comprehension

Unit Three

Directions: Write your Reading Comprehension score for each lesson in the box under the number of the lesson. Then plot your score on the graph by putting a small X on the line directly above the number of the lesson and across from the score you earned. As you mark your score for each lesson, graph your progress by drawing a line to connect the X's.

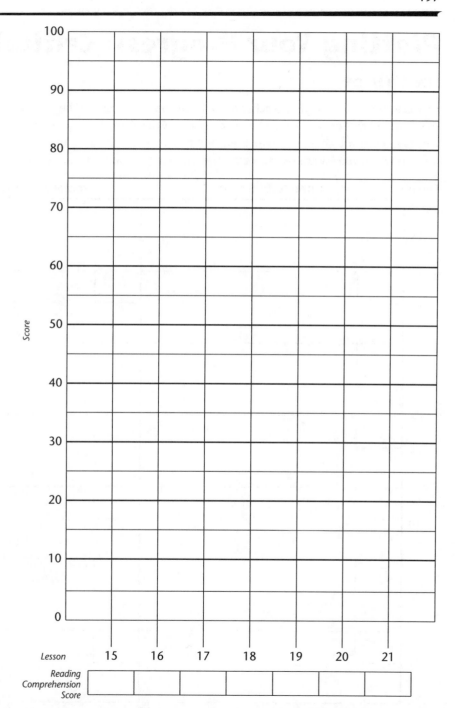

Lesson	15	16	17	18	19	20	21
Reading Comprehension Score							

Plotting Your Progress: Critical Thinking

Unit Three

Directions: Work with your teacher to evaluate your responses to the Critical Thinking questions for each lesson. Then fill in the appropriate spaces in the chart below. For each lesson and each type of Critical Thinking question, do the following: Mark a minus sign (–) in the box to indicate areas in which you feel you could improve. Mark a plus sign (+) to indicate areas in which you feel you did well. Mark a minus-slash-plus sign (–/+) to indicate areas in which you had mixed success. Then write any comments you have about your performance, including ideas for improvement.

Lesson	Author's Approach	Summarizing and Paraphrasing	Critical Thinking
15			
16			
17			
18			
19			
20			
21			

Picture Credits

Cover: Photo montage by Karen Christoffersen

Sample Lesson: pp. 3, 5 Oliver Coote, Everett Collection; p. 4 Everett Collection

Unit 1 Opener: p. 13 Corbis-Bettmann

Lesson 1: p. 14 Corbis-Bettmann; p. 15 Erich Lessing from Art Resource

Lesson 2: p. 22 Everett Collection; p. 23 Eleanore Vere Boyle/Mary Evans Picture Library

Lesson 3: p. 30 Corbis-Bettmann; p. 31 Coupland Collection/Mary Evans Picture Library

Lesson 4: p. 38, 39 AP/Wide World Photos

Lesson 5: p. 46 Mary Evans Picture Library; p. 47 Jeffrey W. Lang/Photo Researchers

Lesson 6: p. 54 Mary Evans Picture Library; p. 55 Fortean Picture Library

Lesson 7: pp. 62, 63 New York State Historical Association, Cooperstown, New York

Unit 2 Opener: p. 75 Popperfoto/Archive Photos

Lesson 8: p. 76 Erich Lessing from Art Resource; p. 77 Mary Evans Picture Library

Lesson 9: pp. 84, 85 Everett Collection

Lesson 10: p. 92 Sonia Halliday Photographs; p. 93 Mary Evans Picture Library

Lesson 11: p. 100 Galleria Borghese, Rome, Italy/Canali Photo Bank, Milan/Superstock; p. 101 Erich Lessing/Art Resource

Lesson 12: p. 108 Field Museum/Photo Researchers; p. 109 Popperfoto/Archive Photos

Lesson 13: p. 116 Hans Reinhard/Bruce Coleman Ltd.; p. 117 Stephen Saks/Photo Researchers

Lesson 14: p. 124 AP/Wide World Photos; p. 125 Patricia Caulfield/Photo Researchers

Unit 3 Opener: p. 137 Corbis-Bettmann

Lesson 15: pp. 138, 139 The Granger Collection

Lesson 16: p. 146 John Sibbick & Fortean Times/Fortean Picture Library; p. 147 Jeff Greenberg/Index Stock Imagery

Lesson 17: p. 154 The Granger Collection; 155 The Kobal Collection

Lesson 18: pp. 162, 163 Lannis Waters/The *Palm Beach Post*

Lesson 19: pp. 170, 171 Mary Evans Picture Library

Lesson 20: p. 178 Debbie Lee/Fortean Picture Library; p. 179 AP/Wide World Photos

Lesson 21: p. 186 Corbis-Bettmann; p. 187 Tom McHugh/Photo Researchers